D0606409

HERSHEY'S®

BEST

Cakes

HERSHEY'S

BEST

Cakes

WILTON HOUSE

Wilton House is an imprint of Joshua Morris Publishing, Inc.

Produced by Joshua Morris Publishing, Inc., 221 Danbury Rd.,
Wilton, CT 06897

All recipes developed and tested in the Hershey Kitchens.
Designed by Marjorie Anderson.
All photographs, with the exception of pages 37, 41,43, 52,
54, 71, 83, 85, 89, 91, 93, 101, and 118 by Bob Skalkowski.
Prop styling for these photographs, except page 41, by Richard
H. Bach.

Trademarks of Hershey Foods Corporation, Joshua Morris Publishing,
Inc., licensee.
Copyright © 1992 Hershey Foods Corporation, Hershey, Pennsylvania.
All rights reserved.
Printed in Canada.
No portion of this book may be reprinted or reproduced in any form or
manner without the written permission of the publishers, except by a
reviewer who wishes to quote brief passages in connection with a review.
First Edition

ISBN: 0-88705-646-6

The delicate combinations of flour, sugar, butter and moisture seem almost endless. Add nuts, fruits, and flavorings and the list of variations grows even longer. But nothing stimulates the senses to try a new recipe as the addition of chocolate.

Chocolate cakes have been a tradition at Hershey since our earliest recipes were recorded. Where else but in Hershey, Pennsylvania would the addition of cocoa or chocolate be as natural an ingredient as flour in cakes. For over 60 years Hershey has been providing consumers with tested and delicious cake recipes. And now the Hershey Kitchens have searched their files, tested and taste paneled their favorite recipes to present to you *HERSHEY'S Best Cakes.*

You'll find cakes for different occasions and seasons. Classic Cakes like "Old-Fashioned Chocolate Cake" and "Chocolatetown Special Cake," Harvest Cakes using the best of the fall harvest with ingredients such as pumpkin, apples and carrots, Cheesecakes using rich dairy cheeses and a variety of great Hershey products, Celebration Cakes to honor special occasions and events such as weddings, birthdays and holidays and even Kids Cakes such as "Chocolate Stripe Cake" to celebrate the kid in each of us are included in this special collection of recipes. The finishing touch to make these cakes look as good as they taste is found in our special Garnish section.

We hope you will enjoy these recipes as much as we do. So celebrate your next special occasion or even your next family meal with a memorable homemade cake from *HERSHEY'S Best Cakes.*

Baking cakes is not difficult nor excessively time consuming. Measuring accurately and following the recipe are the two most important steps in successful cake baking. In order to assist you in making the most of cake baking, the Hershey Kitchens recommend the following:

■ Double check the accuracy of your oven. Use a mercury thermometer to check the temperature. Ovens should have no more than a 25° swing in temperature. Preheating the oven is especially important in cake baking because they require even temperatures.

■ Become familiar with your oven's heating patterns. Usually the center rack of an oven will produce the most even heating pattern but not always. Sometimes the back of the oven will be hotter than the front so you may need to rotate the cake pans for more even heating. Do not place baking sheets on lower oven racks since this will interfere with even heat distribution.

■ Measure accurately using dry and liquid measuring cups. Nested measuring cups should be used for dry ingredients. Lightly spoon flour, cocoa and other dry ingredients into these measuring cups and then level the top with a spatula or knife. Do not pack any ingredient other than brown sugar. Liquid measuring cups, usually glass or translucent plastic should be used for any liquid ingredient. Liquid ingredients should be poured into the cup and the cup should be held at eye level to check the accuracy of the amount.

■ To ensure easy removal of cakes from pans, grease pans generously with shortening and coat with flour; tap out any excess flour. Follow directions for cooling and removing cakes from pans. Cooling racks should always be used. Cakes cooled on a solid surface can be soggy.

Classic Cakes

Deep Dark Chocolate Cake

Deep Dark Chocolate Cake

Heat oven to 350°F. Grease and flour two 9-inch round baking pans or one 13 x 9 x 2-inch baking pan. In large mixer bowl, stir together sugar, flour, cocoa, baking powder, baking soda and salt. Add eggs, milk, oil and vanilla; beat on medium speed of electric mixer 2 minutes. Remove from mixer; stir in boiling water (batter will be thin). Pour batter into prepared pans. Bake 30 to 35 minutes for round pans, 35 to 40 minutes for rectangular pan or until wooden pick inserted in center comes out clean. Cool 10 minutes; remove from pans to wire racks. Cool completely. (Cake may be left in rectangular pan, if desired.) Frost with One-Bowl Buttercream Frosting. 8 to 10 servings.

ONE-BOWL BUTTERCREAM FROSTING: In small mixer bowl, beat butter. Add powdered sugar and cocoa alternately with milk; beat to spreading consistency (additional milk may be needed). Blend in vanilla. About 2 cups frosting.

2 cups sugar
1¾ cups all-purpose flour
¾ cup HERSHEY'S Cocoa or HERSHEY'S Premium European Style Cocoa
1½ teaspoons baking powder
1½ teaspoons baking soda
1 teaspoon salt
2 eggs
1 cup milk
½ cup vegetable oil
2 teaspoons vanilla extract
1 cup boiling water
One-Bowl Buttercream Frosting

One-Bowl Buttercream Frosting
6 tablespoons butter or margarine, softened
2⅔ cups powdered sugar
½ cup HERSHEY'S Cocoa or HERSHEY'S Premium European Style Cocoa
⅓ cup milk
1 teaspoon vanilla extract

European Mocha Fudge Cake, Chocolatetown Chocolate Chip Cake

European Mocha Fudge Cake

Heat oven to 350°F. Butter bottom and sides of two 9-inch round baking pans. Line bottoms with wax paper; butter paper. In small saucepan, melt 1¼ cups butter; remove from heat. Stir in cocoa, blending well; cool slightly. In large mixer bowl, beat eggs until foamy; add salt and vanilla. Gradually add sugar, beating well. Add cooled chocolate mixture; blend thoroughly. Fold in flour. Stir in pecans. Pour batter into prepared pans. Bake 20 to 25 minutes or until wooden pick inserted in center comes out clean. Do *not* overbake. Cool 5 minutes; remove from pans. Carefully peel off paper. Cool completely. Spread Creamy Coffee Filling between layers, over top and sides of cake. Garnish with chocolate curls, if desired. Refrigerate 1 hour or longer before serving. 10 to 12 servings.

CREAMY COFFEE FILLING: In small mixer bowl, combine all ingredients; stir until coffee is almost dissolved. Beat until stiff. About 3 cups filling.

MAKE AHEAD DIRECTIONS: Cooled cake may be wrapped and frozen up to 4 weeks; thaw, wrapped, before filling and frosting.

1¼ cups (2½ sticks) butter or margarine
¾ cup HERSHEY'S Premium European Style Cocoa
4 eggs
¼ teaspoon salt
1 teaspoon vanilla extract
2 cups sugar
1 cup all-purpose flour
1 cup finely chopped pecans
Creamy Coffee Filling
Chocolate curls (optional)

Creamy Coffee Filling
1½ cups cold whipping cream
⅓ cup packed light brown sugar
½ to 1 teaspoon powdered instant coffee

Chocolatetown Chocolate Chip Cake

3 cups all-purpose flour

2 teaspoons baking powder

½ teaspoon salt

1 cup (2 sticks) butter or
   margarine, softened

1 cup granulated sugar

1 cup packed light brown sugar

1½ teaspoons vanilla extract

3 eggs

1 cup milk

1½ cups HERSHEY'S MINI
   CHIPS Semi-Sweet Chocolate

Satiny Mini Chips Glaze

Satiny Mini Chips Glaze

   2 tablespoons sugar

   2 tablespoons water

   ½ cup HERSHEY'S MINI
      CHIPS Semi-Sweet Chocolate

Heat oven to 350°F. Grease and flour 12-cup fluted tube pan or 13 x 9 x 2-inch baking pan. In medium bowl, stir together flour, baking powder and salt. In large mixer bowl, beat together butter, granulated sugar, brown sugar and vanilla until light and fluffy. Add eggs, one at a time, beating well after each addition. Add flour mixture alternately with milk to butter mixture, beating well after each addition. Stir in small chocolate chips. Pour into prepared pan. Bake 55 to 60 minutes for fluted tube pan and 45 to 50 minutes for rectangular pan or until wooden pick inserted in center comes out clean. Cool 15 minutes; remove cake from pan to wire rack. Cool completely. Glaze with Satiny Mini Chips Glaze. 10 to 12 servings.

SATINY MINI CHIPS GLAZE: In small saucepan, combine sugar and water. Heat to boiling; stir until sugar is dissolved. Remove from heat. Immediately add chocolate chips, stirring until melted. Stir until desired consistency. About ½ cup glaze.

BAKER'S HINT

Bloom, the gray-white film that sometimes appears on chocolate chips and bars, occurs when chocolate is exposed to varying temperature. It does not affect the taste or quality of chocolate

Triple Layer Chocolate Mousse Cake

Heat oven to 350°F. Grease and flour three 8-inch round baking pans. In large mixer bowl, stir together sugar, flour, cocoa, baking powder, baking soda and salt. Add eggs, milk, oil and vanilla; beat on medium speed of electric mixer 2 minutes. Remove from mixer; stir in boiling water (batter will be thin). Pour batter into prepared pans. Bake 30 to 35 minutes or until wooden pick inserted in center cones out clean. Cool 10 minutes; remove from pans to wire racks. Cool completely. Prepare Chocolate Mousse. Fill and frost layers with mousse. Garnish with almonds and chocolate curls, if desired. Refrigerate at least 1 hour. Cover; refrigerate leftovers. 10 to 12 servings.

CHOCOLATE MOUSSE: In small bowl, sprinkle gelatin over cold water; let stand 1 minute to soften. Add boiling water; stir until gelatin is completely dissolved and mixture is clear. Cool slightly. In large cold mixer bowl, stir together sugar and cocoa; add whipping cream and vanilla. Beat on medium speed of electric mixer, scraping bottom of bowl occasionally, until stiff; pour in gelatin mixture and beat until well blended. Refrigerate about ½ hour. About 4 cups.

2 cups sugar
1¾ all-purpose flour
¾ HERSHEY'S Cocoa or HERSHEY'S Premium European Style Cocoa
1½ teaspoons baking powder
1½ teaspoons baking soda
1 teaspoon salt
2 eggs
1 cup milk
½ vegetable oil
2 teaspoons vanilla extract
1 cup boiling water
Chocolate Mousse
Sliced almonds (optional)
Chocolate curls (optional)

Chocolate Mousse
1 envelope unflavored gelatin
2 tablespoons cold water
¼ cup boiling water
1 cup sugar
½ cup HERSHEY'S Cocoa
2 cups (1 pt.) cold whipping cream
2 teaspoons vanilla extract

Chocolate Pear Upside–Down Cake

Chocolate Pear Upside–Down Cake

Heat oven to 350°F. In 8-inch square baking pan, melt 3 tablespoons butter in oven. Remove from oven. Add brown sugar; mix well. Spread evenly over bottom of pan. Slice each pear half in two; place in sunburst design over mixture in pan. Arrange nuts and cherries in decorative design between pear sections and in center. Set aside. In large mixer bowl, stir together flour, granulated sugar, cocoa, baking soda and salt. Add remaining 4 tablespoons butter, sour cream, eggs and vanilla; beat on low speed of electric mixer until blended. Beat on medium speed 2 minutes, scraping bowl occasionally. Pour batter into pan over fruit and nuts. Bake 45 to 50 minutes or until wooden pick inserted in center comes out clean. Cool cake in pan on wire rack 5 minutes. Loosen sides and invert cake onto serving plate. Serve warm or cold. 9 to 12 servings.

7 tablespoons butter or margarine, softened and divided
⅓ cup packed light brown sugar
1 can (16 oz.) pear halves (about 4 halves)
¼ cup chopped nuts
Maraschino cherries
1 cup all-purpose flour
1 cup granulated sugar
⅓ cup HERSHEY'S Cocoa
¾ teaspoon baking soda
¼ teaspoon salt
¾ cup dairy sour cream
2 eggs
1 teaspoon vanilla extract

Classic Hershey Bar Cake

1 cup (2 sticks) butter or
  margarine, softened
1¼ cups granulated sugar
4 eggs
6 HERSHEY'S Milk Chocolate
  Bars (1.55 oz. each), melted
2½ cups all-purpose flour
¼ teaspoon baking soda
Dash salt
1 cup buttermilk or sour milk*
½ cup (5½ oz. can) HERSHEY'S
  Syrup
2 teaspoons vanilla extract
1 cup chopped pecans
Powdered sugar (optional)

Heat oven to 350°F. Grease and flour 10-inch tube pan or 12-cup fluted tube pan. In large mixer bowl, beat butter until creamy; gradually add granulated sugar, beating on medium speed of electric mixer until well blended. Add eggs, one at a time, beating well after each addition. Add chocolate; beat until blended. Stir together flour, baking soda and salt; add to chocolate mixture alternately with buttermilk , beating until blended. Add syrup and vanilla; beat until blended. Stir in pecans. Pour batter into prepared pan. Bake 1 hour and 15 minutes or until wooden pick inserted in center of cake comes out clean. Cool 10 minutes; remove from pan to wire rack. Cool completely. Sift powdered sugar over top, if desired. 12 to 16 servings.

* To sour milk: Use 1 tablespoon white vinegar plus milk to equal 1 cup.

BAKER'S HINT

Use fresh ingredients in cake baking, especially spices, baking soda and baking powder. To determine if baking powder is fresh, spoon 1 teaspoonful into ½ cup warm water. If it bubbles, the baking powder is fresh.

Sour Cream Chocolate Cake

Heat oven to 350°F. Grease and flour two 9-inch round baking pans. In small bowl, combine cocoa and water; stir until smooth. Set aside. In large mixer bowl, beat butter until creamy. Add granulated sugar, brown sugar and vanilla; beat until light and fluffy. Add eggs; beat well. Stir in cocoa mixture. Stir together flour, baking powder, baking soda and salt; add alternately with sour cream to butter mixture, beating just until blended. Pour batter into prepared pans. Bake 30 to 35 minutes or until wooden pick inserted in center comes out clean. Cool 15 minutes; remove from pans to wire racks. Cool completely. Frost with Quick Fudge Frosting. 8 to 10 servings.

QUICK FUDGE FROSTING: In small saucepan, heat cream until bubbles form around edge of pan; remove from heat. Set aside. In small mixer bowl, beat butter until creamy. Stir together powdered sugar, cocoa and salt; add alternately with cream to butter, beating to spreading consistency. Blend in vanilla. About 2 cups frosting.

½ cup HERSHEY'S Cocoa
½ cup hot water
½ cup (1 stick) butter or margarine, softened
1 cup granulated sugar
½ cup packed light brown sugar
1½ teaspoons vanilla extract
3 eggs
1¾ cups all-purpose flour
1½ teaspoons baking powder
1 teaspoon baking soda
1 teaspoon salt
1 cup (8 oz.) dairy sour cream
Quick Fudge Frosting

Quick Fudge Frosting
6 to 7 tablespoons light cream or evaporated milk
⅓ cup butter or margarine, softened
3 cups powdered sugar
6 tablespoons HERSHEY'S Cocoa
⅛ teaspoon salt
1 teaspoon vanilla extract

Chocolate Lemon Marble Cake

2½ cups all-purpose flour

1¾ cups plus ⅓ cup sugar,
   divided

2 teaspoons baking powder

1¼ teaspoons baking soda,
   divided

½ teaspoon salt

⅓ cup butter or margarine,
   softened

⅓ cup shortening

3 eggs

1⅔ cups buttermilk or sour milk*

2 teaspoons vanilla extract

⅓ cup HERSHEY'S Cocoa

¼ cup water

2 teaspoons freshly grated
   lemon peel

¼ teaspoon lemon extract

Cocoa Glaze

Cocoa Glaze
   ¼ cup HERSHEY'S Cocoa
   3 tablespoons light corn syrup
   4 teaspoons water
   ½ teaspoon vanilla extract
   1 cup powdered sugar

Heat oven to 375°F. Grease and flour two 9 x 5 x 3-inch loaf pans. In large mixer bowl, stir together flour, 1¾ cups sugar, baking powder, 1 teaspoon baking soda and salt. Add butter, shortening, eggs, buttermilk and vanilla; beat on medium speed of electric mixer 3 minutes. Stir together cocoa, remaining ⅓ cup sugar, remaining ¼ teaspoon baking soda and water; blend into ⅔ cup vanilla batter. Blend lemon peel and lemon extract into remaining vanilla batter. Spoon lemon batter into prepared pans; dollop chocolate batter onto top of lemon batter. Swirl with spatula for marbled effect. Bake 40 to 45 minutes or until wooden pick inerted in center comes out clean. Cool 15 minutes; remove from pans to wire rack. Cool completely. Glaze with Cocoa Glaze. 16 to 18 servings.

COCOA GLAZE: In small saucepan, combine cocoa, corn syrup and water. Cook over medium heat, stirring constantly, until mixture thickens. Remove from heat; blend in vanilla and powdered sugar. Beat until smooth.

* To sour milk: Use 1 tablespoon plus 2 teaspoons white vinegar plus milk to equal 1⅔ cups.

Chocolate Lemon Marble, Chocolate Rum Pecan Pound Cake

Chocolate Rum Pecan Pound Cake

⅔ cup HERSHEY'S Cocoa,
  divided
¼ cup boiling water
1¼ cups (2½ sticks) butter or
  margarine, softened
2⅔ cups sugar
1 teaspoon vanilla extract
5 eggs
2 cups all-purpose flour
1 teaspoon salt
½ teaspoon baking powder
¼ teaspoon baking soda
½ cup buttermilk or sour milk*
¾ cup finely chopped pecans
¼ cup light rum *or* 1½ teaspoons
  rum extract plus ¼ cup water
Chocolate Glaze

Chocolate Glaze
  3 tablespoons butter or
    margarine
  3 tablespoons light corn syrup
  1 tablespoon water
  1 cup HERSHEY'S Semi-Sweet
    Chocolate Chips

Heat oven to 325°F. Grease and flour 12-cup fluted tube pan. In small bowl, stir ⅓ cup cocoa and water until smooth; set aside. In large mixer bowl, beat butter, sugar and vanilla until creamy. Add eggs, one at a time, beating well after each addition. Add reserved cocoa mixture; beat well. Stir together flour, remaining ⅓ cup cocoa, salt, baking powder and baking soda; add to butter mixture alternately with buttermilk , beating until well blended. Stir in pecans and rum. Pour batter into prepared pan. Bake 1 hour and 5 minutes or until wooden pick inserted in center of cake comes out clean. Cool 10 minutes; remove from pan to wire rack. Cool completely. Drizzle Chocolate Glaze over cake. 10 to 12 servings.

CHOCOLATE GLAZE: In small saucepan, combine butter, corn syrup and water. Cook over medium heat, stirring constantly, until mixture begins to boil. Remove from heat; add chocolate chips, stirring until melted. Cool slightly.

* To sour milk: Use 1½ teaspoons white vinegar plus milk to equal ½ cup.

Cocoa Medallion Cake

Heat oven to 350°F. Grease two 9-inch round baking pans; line bottoms with wax paper. In bowl, stir together cocoa and water until smooth; set aside. In large mixer bowl, beat butter, shortening and sugar until well blended. Add eggs, vanilla and salt; beat well. In separate bowl, stir baking soda into buttermilk ; add alternately with flour to butter mixture, beginning and ending with flour. Add cocoa mixture; blend thoroughly. Pour batter into prepared pans. Bake 30 to 35 minutes or until wooden pick inserted in center comes out clean. Cool 10 minutes; remove from pans to wire racks. Cool completely. Frost as desired. 10 to 12 servings.

VARIATION
PICNIC MEDALLION CAKE: Prepare batter as directed above; pour into greased and floured 13 x 9 x 2-inch baking pan. Bake at 350°F 40 to 45 minutes or until wooden pick inserted in center comes out clean. Cool completely; frost as desired.

* To sour milk: Use 1 tablespoon white vinegar plus milk to equal 1 cup.

¾ cup HERSHEY'S Cocoa
¾ cup boiling water
¼ cup (½ stick) butter or margarine, softened
¼ cup shortening
2 cups sugar
2 eggs
1 teaspoon vanilla extract
⅛ teaspoon salt
1½ teaspoons baking soda
1 cup buttermilk or sour milk*
1¾ cups all-purpose flour

Fresh Coconut Cake with Dark Chocolate Frosting

1¾ cups sugar

½ cup vegetable oil

3 eggs

1 teaspoon vanilla extract

2 cups all-purpose flour

3 teaspoons baking powder

½ teaspoon salt

1 cup coconut milk or milk

1 cup grated fresh coconut*

Dark Chocolate Frosting

¾ cup grated fresh coconut **
  (optional)

Dark Chocolate Frosting

  6 tablespoons butter or
    margarine, softened

  2⅔ cups powdered sugar

  ¾ cup HERSHEY'S Cocoa

  4 to 5 tablespoons milk

  1 teaspoon vanilla extract

Heat oven to 350°F. Grease and flour two 9-inch round baking pans. In large mixer bowl, beat sugar and oil; add eggs and vanilla, beating until well blended. Stir together flour, baking powder and salt; add alternately with coconut milk to sugar mixture, beating until batter is smooth. Stir in 1 cup coconut. Pour batter into prepared pans. Bake 35 to 40 minutes or until wooden pick inserted in center comes out clean. Cool 10 minutes; remove from pans to wire racks. Cool completely. Frost with Dark Chocolate Frosting. Sprinkle ¾ cup coconut over top, if desired. 8 to 10 servings.

DARK CHOCOLATE FROSTING: In small mixer bowl, beat butter until creamy. Gradually add powdered sugar and cocoa alternately with milk and vanilla, beating to spreading consistency. About 2 cups frosting.

* If fresh coconut is not available, packaged, flaked coconut can be substituted.

** Sweetened by stirring in 2 tablespoons powdered sugar.

Fresh Coconut Cake with Dark Chocolate Frosting

Collector's Cocoa Cake

Heat oven to 350°F. Grease and flour two 8- or 9-inch round baking pans. In large mixer bowl, beat butter and sugar until light and fluffy. Add eggs and vanilla; beat on medium speed of electric mixer 1 minute. Stir together flour, cocoa, baking soda and salt; add to butter mixture alternately with water, beating after each addition. Pour batter into prepared pans. Bake 35 to 40 minutes for 8-inch rounds, 30 to 35 minutes for 9-inch rounds or until wooden pick inserted in center comes out clean. Cool 10 minutes; remove from pans to wire racks. Cool completely. Frost with Fluffy Peanut Butter Frosting. 8 to 10 servings.

FLUFFY PEANUT BUTTER FROSTING: In small saucepan, gradually stir milk into flour. Cook over low heat, stirring constantly, until very thick. Transfer to small mixer bowl; place plastic wrap directly on surface. Cool to room temperature. Add peanut butter, shortening, sugar, vanilla and salt. Beat on high speed of electric mixer until mixture becomes fluffy and sugar is completely dissolved. About 3 cups frosting.

¾ cup (1½ sticks) butter or
   margarine, softened
1¾ cups sugar
2 eggs
1 teaspoon vanilla extract
2 cups all-purpose flour
¾ cup HERSHEY'S Cocoa or
   HERSHEY'S Premium
   European Style Cocoa
1¼ teaspoons baking soda
½ teaspoon salt
1⅓ cups water
Fluffy Peanut Butter Frosting

Fluffy Peanut Butter Frosting
   1 cup milk
   3 tablespoons all-purpose flour
   ½ cup REESE'S Creamy
      Peanut Butter
   ½ cup shortening
   1 cup sugar
   1 teaspoon vanilla extract
   Dash salt

Collector's Cocoa Cake

Chocolate Cherry Upside–Down Cake

1 tablespoon cold water

1 tablespoon cornstarch

¼ to ½ teaspoon almond extract
  (optional)

1 can (21 oz.) cherry pie filling

1⅔ cups all-purpose flour

1 cup sugar

¼ cup HERSHEY'S Cocoa

1 teaspoon baking soda

½ teaspoon salt

1 cup water

⅓ cup vegetable oil

1 teaspoon white vinegar

½ teaspoon vanilla extract

Sweetened whipped cream

Heat oven to 350°F. In bowl, stir together 1 tablespoon water, cornstarch and almond extract, if desired, until cornstarch is dissolved. Stir in pie filling; blend well. Spread mixture evenly on bottom of ungreased 9-inch square baking pan; set aside. Stir together flour, sugar, cocoa, baking soda and salt. Add 1 cup water, oil, vinegar and vanilla; beat with spoon or wire whisk until batter is smooth and well blended. Pour batter evenly over cherries. Bake 40 to 45 minutes or until wooden pick inserted in center comes out clean. Cool 10 minutes; invert onto serving plate. Serve warm with sweetened whipped cream. About 9 servings.

Chocolate Filled Graham Roll

Heat oven to 400°F. Line 15½ x 10½ x 1-inch jelly roll pan with foil; generously grease foil. In small bowl, stir together graham cracker crumbs, flour and baking powder. In large bowl, beat egg yolks, ¼ cup sugar, water and vanilla until thick and lemon colored, about 5 minutes. In second large bowl, beat egg whites until foamy; gradually add remaining ¼ cup sugar, continuing to beat until stiff. Fold egg white mixture into egg yolk mixture. Carefully fold in flour mixture. Fold in butter. Immediately pour batter into prepared pan, spreading evenly. Bake 12 to 15 minutes or until top springs back when touched lightly in center. Loosen cake from edges of pan; invert onto towel sprinkled with powdered sugar. Carefully peel off foil. Immediately roll cake and towel from narrow end. Cool on wire rack 30 minutes. Unroll cake; remove towel. Reroll without towel; cool completely. Unroll cake; spread with Chocolate Cream Filling. Reroll and refrigerate. Sprinkle powdered sugar over top or glaze with Chocolate Glaze. 8 to 10 servings.

CHOCOLATE CREAM FILLING: In small mixer bowl, combine sugar and cocoa. Add whipping cream and vanilla. Beat on low speed of electric mixer until smooth, about 30 seconds; beat on medium speed until stiff.

CHOCOLATE GLAZE: In small saucepan, combine butter, water and cocoa. Cook over low heat, stirring constantly, until butter melts and mixture thickens. Do *not* boil. Remove from heat; stir in powdered sugar and vanilla extract. Pour warm glaze on top of cakeroll, allowing glaze to run down sides. Spread with spatula to completely glaze roll.

1 cup graham cracker crumbs
¼ cup all-purpose flour
1 teaspoon baking powder
4 eggs, separated
½ cup sugar, divided
¼ cup water
1 teaspoon vanilla extract
2 tablespoons butter or margarine, melted
Chocolate Cream Filling
Powdered sugar or Chocolate Glaze

Chocolate Cream Filling
  ½ cup sugar
  ¼ cup HERSHEY'S Cocoa
  1 cup (½ pt.) cold whipping cream
  1 teaspoon vanilla extract

Chocolate Glaze
  2 tablespoons butter or margarine
  2 tablespoons water
  2 tablespoons HERSHEY'S Cocoa
  1 cup powdered sugar
  ½ teaspoon vanilla extract

Red Velvet Cocoa Cake

½ cup (1 stick) butter or
   margarine, softened
1½ cups sugar
1 teaspoon vanilla extract
2 eggs
1 tablespoon red food color
2 cups all-purpose flour
¼ cup HERSHEY'S Cocoa
1 teaspoon salt
1 cup buttermilk or sour milk*
1½ teaspoons baking soda
1 tablespoon white vinegar
Fluffy Vanilla Frosting

Fluffy Vanilla Frosting
   ½ cup (1 stick) butter or
      margarine, softened
   5 cups powdered sugar, divided
   2 teaspoons vanilla extract
   ⅛ teaspoon salt
   4 to 5 tablespoons milk

Heat oven to 350°F. Grease and flour two 9-inch round baking pans. In large mixer bowl, beat butter, sugar and vanilla until creamy. Add eggs and food color; blend well. Stir together flour, cocoa and salt; add alternately with buttermilk to butter mixture. Stir baking soda into vinegar; fold carefully into batter (do not beat). Pour batter into prepared pans. Bake 30 to 35 minutes or until wooden pick inserted in center comes out clean. Cool 10 minutes; remove from pans to wire racks. Cool completely. Frost with Fluffy Vanilla Frosting. 10 to 12 servings.

FLUFFY VANILLA FROSTING: In large mixer bowl, beat butter, 1 cup powdered sugar, vanilla and salt. Add remaining powdered sugar alternately with milk, beating to spreading consistency. About 2½ cups frosting.

* To sour milk: Use 1 tablespoon white vinegar plus milk to equal 1 cup.

Red Velvet Cocoa Cake

Hershey's Semi—Sweet Chocolate Torte

6 bars (6 oz.) HERSHEY'S Semi-
  Sweet Baking Chocolate,
  broken into pieces
¾ cup (1½ sticks) butter or
  margarine, softened
1½ cups sugar
2 eggs
2 teaspoons vanilla extract
2¼ cups all-purpose flour
1 teaspoon baking soda
½ teaspoon salt
1¼ cups water
Chocolate Cream Filling
Semi-Sweet Royal Glaze

Chocolate Cream Filling
  2 bars (2 oz.) HERSHEY'S
    Semi-Sweet Baking Chocolate
  ¼ cup milk
  1 package (3 oz.) cream cheese,
    softened
  1 cup (½ pt.) cold whipping
    cream
  ¼ cup powdered sugar
  1 teaspoon vanilla extract

Semi-Sweet Royal Glaze
  8 bars (8 oz.) HERSHEY'S
    Semi-Sweet Baking Chocolate

Heat oven to 350°F. Grease two 9-inch round baking pans. Line bottoms with wax paper; grease and flour paper and sides of pans. Melt chocolate; cool to lukewarm. In large mixer bowl, beat butter and sugar until well blended; add eggs and vanilla, beating well. Blend in chocolate. Stir together flour, baking soda and salt; add alternately with water to butter mixture, beating until well blended. Pour batter evenly into prepared pans. Bake 30 to 35 minutes or until wooden pick inserted in center comes out clean. Cool 10 minutes; remove from pans to wire racks. Cool completely. Prepare Chocolate Cream Filling. Spread filling between cake layers, with rounded side up on top layer; refrigerate. Prepare Semi-Sweet Royal Glaze. Pour over top allowing to drip down sides; spread evenly over top and sides of torte. Cover; refrigerate. About 12 servings.

CHOCOLATE CREAM FILLING: In small saucepan over very low heat, melt chocolate with milk, stirring until mixture is smooth and well blended; cool slightly. In small mixer bowl, beat cream cheese until fluffy; gradually blend in chocolate mixture. In separate bowl, beat whipping cream, powdered sugar and vanilla until stiff; fold into chocolate mixture. Refrigerate until firm.

SEMI-SWEET ROYAL GLAZE: In small saucepan over very low heat, melt chocolate, stirring constantly, just until chocolate is melted and mixture is smooth. Remove from heat; cool until thickened and lukewarm, about 15 minutes.

Ice – Itself Chocolate Cake

Heat oven to 350°F. Line 13 x 9 x 2-inch baking pan with foil; butter foil. In small bowl, stir together coconut, pecans, brown sugar, melted butter, evaporated milk and corn syrup. Spread mixture evenly over bottom of pan. In large mixer bowl, beat softened butter and granulated sugar until light and fluffy. Add egg and vanilla; beat well. Stir together flour, cocoa, baking soda, baking powder and salt; add to beaten butter mixture alternately with milk. Carefully spread batter in prepared pan; do not mix with coconut layer. Bake 35 to 40 minutes or until top springs back when touched lightly. Invert immediately onto wire rack; gently remove foil and discard. Cover layer loosely with another piece of foil to keep topping soft. Cool completely. Keep well covered. 12 to 15 servings.

1 cup flaked coconut
½ cup chopped pecans
⅓ cup packed light brown sugar
3 tablespoons butter or margarine, melted
3 tablespoons evaporated milk
2 tablespoons light corn syrup
½ cup (1 stick) butter or margarine, softened
1 cup plus 2 tablespoons granulated sugar
1 egg
½ teaspoon vanilla extract
1¼ cups plus 2 tablespoons all-purpose flour
⅓ cup HERSHEY'S Cocoa
1 teaspoon baking soda
¼ teaspoon baking powder
½ teaspoon salt
1 cup milk

Quick 'n' Easy Chocolate Cupcakes

2 cups all-purpose flour

1½ cups sugar

⅔ cup HERSHEY'S Cocoa

2 teaspoons baking powder

½ teaspoon baking soda

½ teaspoon salt

⅔ cup shortening

2 eggs

⅔ cup milk

½ cup hot water

1½ teaspoons vanilla extract

Creamy Fudge Frosting

Creamy Fudge Frosting

  ½ cup (1 stick) butter or
    margarine

  ½ cup HERSHEY'S Cocoa

  3⅔ cups (1 lb.) powdered sugar

  1½ teaspoons vanilla extract

  Dash salt

  ⅓ cup water

Heat oven to 350°F. Paper-line 30 muffin cups (2½ inches in diameter). In large mixer bowl, stir together flour, sugar, cocoa, baking powder, baking soda and salt. Add shortening, eggs, milk, water and vanilla; beat 1 minute on low speed of electric mixer. Beat additional 3 minutes on medium speed or until mixture is smooth and creamy. Spoon batter into prepared cups, filling each cup about half full. Bake 15 to 20 minutes or until center of cupcake springs back when touched lightly in center. Remove cupcakes from pan to wire rack. Cool completely. (Do not cool cupcakes in pan; paper liners will come loose from cupcakes.) Prepare Creamy Fudge Frosting. Frost cooled cupcakes. 30 cupcakes.

CREAMY FUDGE FROSTING: In medium saucepan over low heat, melt butter. Add cocoa; stir until smooth and well blended. Remove from heat. Add powdered sugar, vanilla and salt alternately with water; beat with spoon or wire whisk until smooth and creamy. Additional water, ½ teaspoon at a time, may be added, if frosting becomes too thick. About 2 cups frosting.

Quick 'n' Easy Cupcakes, One Bowl Chocolate Cake

One Bowl Chocolate Cake

⅔ cup butter or margarine,
   softened
1¾ cups sugar
2 cups all-purpose flour
½ cup HERSHEY'S Cocoa
2 teaspoons baking powder
½ teaspoon baking soda
½ teaspoon salt
3 eggs
1½ cups milk
1 teaspoon vanilla extract

Heat oven to 350°F. Grease and flour two 8- or 9-inch round baking pans or one 13 x 9 x 2-inch baking pan. In large mixer bowl, beat butter and sugar until well blended. Add remaining ingredients. Beat on low speed of electric mixer 1 minute, scraping bowl constantly. Beat on high speed 2 minutes, scraping bowl and beaters occasionally. Pour batter into prepared pans. Bake 30 to 35 minutes for round pans; 40 to 45 minutes for rectangular pan or until wooden pick inserted in center comes out clean. Cool 10 minutes; remove from pans to wire racks. Cool completely. (Cake may be left in rectangular pan, if desired.) Frost as desired. 8 to 12 servings.

BAKER'S HINT

Butter and margarine are usually interchangeable if both are listed in the ingredient list. Use the stick variety rather than soft or tub butter or margarine. Do not substitute shortening because the texture and moisture will be affected. Diet, "light," or lower fat products , and "spreads" act differently in cooking and baking than regular butter or stick margarine and may cause unsatisfactory results.

Chocolatetown Special Cake

Heat oven to 350°F. Grease and flour two 9-inch round baking pans. In small bowl, stir together cocoa and water until smooth; set aside. In large mixer bowl, beat shortening, sugar and vanilla until light and fluffy. Add eggs; beat well. Stir together flour, baking soda and salt; add to shortening mixture alternately with buttermilk . Blend in cocoa mixture; beat well. Pour batter into prepared pans. Bake 35 to 40 minutes or until wooden pick inserted in center comes out clean. Cool 10 minutes; remove from pans to wire rack. Cool completely. Frost with One-Bowl Buttercream Frosting. 8 to 10 servings.

ONE-BOWL BUTTERCREAM FROSTING: In small mixer bowl, beat butter. Add powdered sugar and cocoa alternately with milk; beat to spreading consistency (additional milk may be needed). Blend in vanilla. About 2 cups frosting.

* To Sour Milk: Use 4 teaspoons white vinegar plus milk to equal 1⅓ cups.

½ cup HERSHEY'S Cocoa or HERSHEY'S Premium European Style Cocoa
½ cup boiling water
⅔ cup shortening
1¾ cups sugar
1 teaspoon vanilla extract
2 eggs
2 ¼ cups all-purpose flour
1½ teaspoons baking soda
½ teaspoon salt
1⅓ cups buttermilk or sour milk*
One-Bowl Buttercream Frosting

One-Bowl Buttercream Frosting
6 tablespoons butter or margarine, softened
2⅔ cups powdered sugar
½ cup HERSHEY'S Cocoa or HERSHEY'S Premium European Style Cocoa
⅓ cup milk
1 teaspoon vanilla extract

Classic Boston Cream Pie

⅓ cup shortening

1 cup sugar

2 eggs

1 teaspoon vanilla extract

1¼ cups all-purpose flour

1½ teaspoons baking powder

¼ teaspoon salt

¾ cup milk

Rich Filling

Dark Cocoa Glaze

Rich Filling

⅓ cup sugar

2 tablespoons cornstarch

1½ cups milk

2 egg yolks, slightly beaten

1 tablespoon butter or
  margarine

1 teaspoon vanilla extract

Dark Cocoa Glaze

3 tablespoons water

2 tablespoons butter or
  margarine

3 tablespoons HERSHEY'S
  Cocoa

1 cup powdered sugar

½ teaspoon vanilla extract

Heat oven to 350°F. Grease and flour 9-inch round baking pan. In large mixer bowl, beat shortening, sugar, eggs and vanilla until light and fluffy. Stir together flour, baking powder and salt; add alternately with milk to shortening mixture. Pour batter into prepared pan. Bake 30 to 35 minutes or until wooden pick inserted in center comes out clean. Cool 10 minutes; remove from pan to wire rack. Cool completely. Prepare Rich Filling. With long serrated knife, cut cake horizontally into two even layers. Place 1 layer on serving plate, cut side up; spread filling over layer. Top with remaining cake layer, cut side down. Prepare Dark Cocoa Glaze. Pour glaze onto top of cake, allowing some to drizzle down sides. Refrigerate before serving. Refrigerate leftovers. 8 to 10 servings.

RICH FILLING: In medium saucepan, stir together sugar and cornstarch; gradually add milk and egg yolks, stirring until blended. Cook over medium heat, stirring constantly, until mixture boils. Boil and stir 1 minute. Remove from heat; stir in butter and vanilla. Cover; refrigerate several hours until cold.

DARK COCOA GLAZE: In small saucepan, heat water and butter to full boil; remove from heat. Immediately stir in cocoa. Gradually add powdered sugar and vanilla, beating with whisk until smooth; cool slightly.

Classic Boston Cream Pie, Old–Fashioned Chocolate Cake

Old-Fashioned Chocolate Cake

¾ cup (1½ sticks) butter or
   margarine
1⅔ cups sugar
3 eggs
1 teaspoon vanilla extract
2 cups all-purpose flour
⅔ cup HERSHEY'S Cocoa
1¼ teaspoons baking soda
1 teaspoon salt
¼ teaspoon baking powder
1⅓ cups water
½ cup finely crushed hard
   peppermint candy (optional)
One-Bowl Buttercream Frosting
Additional crushed hard
   peppermint candy (optional)

One-Bowl Buttercream Frosting
   6 tablespoons butter or
      margarine, softened
   2⅔ cups powdered sugar
   ½ cup HERSHEY'S Cocoa
   ⅓ cup milk
   1 teaspoon vanilla extract

Heat oven to 350°F. Grease and flour two 9-inch round baking pans or one 13 x 9 x 2-inch baking pan. In large mixer bowl, combine butter, sugar, eggs and vanilla; beat on high speed of electric mixer 3 minutes. In separate bowl, stir together flour, cocoa, baking soda, salt and baking powder; add alternately with water to butter mixture. Blend just until combined; add ½ cup candy, if desired. Pour batter into prepared pans. Bake 30 to 35 minutes or until wooden pick inserted in center comes out clean. Cool 10 minutes; remove from pans to wire racks. Cool completely. Frost with One-Bowl Buttercream Frosting. Just before serving, garnish with peppermint candy, if desired. 8 to 10 servings.

ONE-BOWL BUTTERCREAM FROSTING: In small mixer bowl, beat butter. Add powdered sugar and cocoa alternately with milk; beat to spreading consistency (additional milk may be needed). Blend in vanilla. About 2 cups frosting.

VARIATION
CHOCOLATE CUPCAKES: Fill paper-lined muffin cups (2½ inches in diameter) ⅔ full with batter. Bake at 350°F for 20 to 25 minutes. Cool; frost. About 2½ dozen cupcakes.

Feathery Fudge Cake

Heat oven to 350°F. In small microwave-safe bowl, place chocolate. Microwave at HIGH (100%) 1½ to 2 minutes or until smooth when stirred; set aside to cool slightly. Grease and flour two 9-inch round baking pans. In large mixer bowl, beat butter, sugar and vanilla until light and fluffy. Add eggs and cooled chocolate; blend well. Stir together flour, baking soda and salt; add alternately with water to butter mixture. Pour batter into prepared pans. Bake 35 to 40 minutes or until wooden pick inserted in center comes out clean. Cool in pans 10 minutes; remove from pans to wire racks. Cool completely. Frost with Chocolate Syrup Frosting. Refrigerate 1 hour or longer before serving. Refrigerate leftovers. 10 to 12 servings.

CHOCOLATE SYRUP FROSTING: In large mixer bowl, combine whipping cream, syrup and vanilla. Beat until mixture is of spreading consistency. About 3 cups frosting.

2½ bars (2½ oz.) HERSHEY'S Unsweetened Baking Chocolate, broken into pieces
¾ cup (1½ sticks) butter or margarine, softened
2 cups sugar
1 teaspoon vanilla extract
2 eggs
2¼ cups all-purpose flour
1¼ teaspoons baking soda
½ teaspoon salt
1⅓ cups water
Chocolate Syrup Frosting

Chocolate Syrup Frosting
   1½ cups cold whipping cream
   ⅔ cup HERSHEY'S Syrup, chilled
   ½ teaspoon vanilla extract

1 cup of frosting will frost the top of a 13 x 9-inch cake. 2 cups frosting will fill and frost an 8- or 9-inch two layer cake or 24 cupcakes.

BAKER'S HINT

Black Forest Cake

1⅔ cups all-purpose flour
1½ cups sugar
½ cup HERSHEY'S Cocoa
1½ teaspoons baking soda
½ teaspoon baking powder
1 teaspoon salt
2 eggs
½ cup shortening
1½ cups buttermilk or
  sour milk*
1 teaspoon vanilla extract
Sweetened Whipped Cream
1 can (21 oz.) cherry pie filling
Sliced almonds

Sweetened Whipped Cream
  1½ cups cold whipping
    cream
  3 tablespoons powdered sugar
  ¾ teaspoon vanilla extract

Heat oven to 350°F. Grease and flour two 9-inch round baking pans. In large mixer bowl, stir together flour, sugar, cocoa, baking soda, baking powder and salt; add eggs, shortening, buttermilk and vanilla. Beat on low speed of electric mixer 1 minute, scraping bowl constantly. Beat on high speed 3 minutes, scraping bowl occasionally. Pour batter into prepared pans. Bake 30 to 35 minutes or until wooden pick inserted in center comes out clean. Cool 10 minutes; remove from pans to wire racks. Cool completely. Prepare Sweetened Whipped Cream. Place one cake layer on serving plate. Spoon half of cherry pie filling in center and spread to within ½ inch of edge. Spoon or pipe border of whipped cream around edge. Top with second layer. Spoon remaining cherry pie filling to within ½ inch of edge. Frost sides with whipped cream; spoon or pipe border around top edge. Pat almonds onto sides of cake. Refrigerate. 10 to 12 servings.

SWEETENED WHIPPED CREAM: In small mixer bowl, combine whipping cream, powdered sugar and vanilla extract; beat until stiff.

* To sour milk: Use 4½ teaspoons white vinegar plus milk to equal 1½ cups.

Black Forest Cake

Chocolate Orange Marble Chiffon Cake

⅓ cup HERSHEY'S Cocoa

¼ cup hot water

3 tablespoons plus 1½ cups sugar, divided

2 tablespoons plus ½ cup vegetable oil, divided

2¼ cups all-purpose flour

3 teaspoons baking powder

1 teaspoon salt

¾ cup cold water

7 egg yolks

1 cup egg whites (about 8)

½ teaspoon cream of tartar

1 tablespoon freshly grated orange peel

Orange Glaze

Orange Glaze

⅓ cup butter or margarine

2 cups powdered sugar

2 to 3 tablespoons orange juice

½ teaspoon freshly grated orange peel

Remove top oven rack; move other rack to lowest position. Heat oven to 325°F. In medium bowl, stir together cocoa and hot water; stir in 3 tablespoons sugar and 2 tablespoons oil; set aside. In large bowl, stir together flour, remaining 1½ cups sugar, baking powder and salt. Add in order: cold water, remaining ½ cup oil and egg yolks; beat with spoon until smooth. Set aside. In large mixer bowl, beat egg whites and cream of tartar until very stiff peaks form; pour egg yolk mixture in a thin stream over egg white mixture and gently fold in just until blended. Remove 2 cups batter; add to chocolate mixture, gently folding in until well blended. To remaining batter, fold in orange peel. Spoon half of orange batter into ungreased 10-inch tube pan; dollop with half of chocolate batter. Repeat layers of orange and chocolate batters. With narrow metal spatula, swirl through batters to marble, leaving definite orange and chocolate areas. Bake 1 hour and 15 to 20 minutes or until top springs back when touched lightly. Immediately invert cake in pan on heatproof funnel; cool completely. Remove cake from pan; invert onto serving plate. Spread top of cake with Orange Glaze, allowing some to drizzle down sides. 12 to 16 servings.

ORANGE GLAZE: In medium saucepan over low heat, melt butter. Remove from heat; stir in powdered sugar, orange juice and orange peel until smooth and of desired consistency. About 1½ cups glaze.

Heritage Chocolate Cake, Chocolate Orange Marble Chiffon Cake

Heritage Chocolate Cake

⅔ cup butter or margarine,
  softened
1¾ cups sugar
3 eggs
1 teaspoon vanilla extract
2 cups all-purpose flour
½ cup HERSHEY'S Cocoa
1 teaspoon baking powder
¾ teaspoon baking soda
½ teaspoon salt
1½ cups buttermilk or sour
  milk*
Chocolate Fudge Frosting

Chocolate Fudge Frosting
  ⅓ cup butter or margarine
  ⅓ cup HERSHEY'S Cocoa
  2⅔ cups powdered sugar
  ⅓ cup milk
  1 teaspoon vanilla extract

Heat oven to 350°F. Grease and flour two 9-inch round baking pans. In large mixer bowl, beat butter, sugar, eggs and vanilla until light and fluffy. Stir together flour, cocoa, baking powder, baking soda and salt; add alternately with buttermilk to butter mixture, beating just until smooth. Pour batter into prepared pans. Bake 30 to 35 minutes or until wooden pick inserted in center comes out clean. Cool 10 minutes; remove from pans to wire racks. Cool completely. Frost with Chocolate Fudge Frosting. 8 to 10 servings.

CHOCOLATE FUDGE FROSTING: In small saucepan over low heat, melt butter; add cocoa, stirring constantly until smooth and slightly thickened. Remove from heat; pour into small mixer bowl. Cool completely. Add powdered sugar alternately with milk and vanilla, beating to spreading consistency. About 2 cups frosting.

* To sour milk: Use 4½ teaspoons white vinegar plus milk to equal 1½ cups.

Cheesecakes

Raspberry Chocolate Swirl Cheesecake

Chocolate Crumb Crust

3 packages (8 oz. each) cream
  cheese, softened

1 cup sugar, divided

1½ teaspoons vanilla extract,
  divided

3 eggs

¼ cup HERSHEY'S Cocoa

1 tablespoon vegetable oil

⅔ cup seedless red raspberry
  preserves

3 tablespoons all-purpose flour

Raspberry Sauce

Raspberries (optional)

Chocolate Crumb Crust

  1¼ cups vanilla wafer crumbs
    (about 40 wafers)

  ¼ cup HERSHEY'S Cocoa

  ¼ cup powdered sugar

  ¼ cup (½ stick) butter or
    margarine, melted

Raspberry Sauce

  ¼ cup sugar

  2 teaspoons cornstarch

  1 package (10 oz.) frozen red
    raspberries, thawed

Prepare Chocolate Crumb Crust; set aside. Heat oven to 425°F. In large mixer bowl, beat cream cheese, ¾ cup sugar and 1 teaspoon vanilla until smooth. Add eggs; beat until well blended. In small bowl, stir together cocoa and remaining ¼ cup sugar. Add oil, remaining ½ teaspoon vanilla and 1½ cups cream cheese mixture; blend well. Stir raspberry preserves to soften; add preserves and flour to remaining cream cheese mixture in bowl; blend well. Pour half of raspberry mixture into crust; dollop about half of chocolate mixture onto raspberry. Repeat with remaining batter ending with chocolate dollops on top; gently swirl with knife or metal spatula for marbled effect. Bake 10 minutes. Reduce oven temperature to 250°F; continue baking 55 minutes or until center appears set. Remove pan from oven to wire rack. With knife, loosen cake from side of pan. Cool completely; remove side of pan. Cover; refrigerate. Serve with Raspberry Sauce and raspberries, if desired. 10 to 12 servings.

CHOCOLATE CRUMB CRUST: Heat oven to 350°F. In medium bowl, combine vanilla wafer crumbs, cocoa and powdered sugar. Stir in butter. Press mixture onto bottom and ½ inch up side of 9-inch springform pan. Bake 8 to 10 minutes; cool slightly.

RASPBERRY SAUCE: In small saucepan, stir together sugar and cornstarch; stir in raspberries. Heat to boiling, stirring constantly; boil and stir 1 minute. Cool; press through sieve to remove seeds. About 1 cup sauce.

Raspberry Chocolate Swirl Cheesecake

Black – Eyed Susan Cheesecakes

24 vanilla wafer cookies
2 packages (8 oz. each) cream
    cheese, softened
½ cup sugar
2 eggs
½ teaspoon vanilla extract
1 cup REESE'S Peanut Butter
    Chips
½ cup HERSHEY'S Semi-Sweet
    Chocolate Chips
3 tablespoons butter
Sliced almonds

Heat oven to 350°F. Line muffin pans with foil laminated baking cups (2 inches in diameter). Place one vanilla wafer in bottom of each cup. In large mixer bowl, beat cream cheese and sugar. Add eggs and vanilla; beat well. Stir in peanut butter chips. Spoon heaping tablespoonful cream cheese mixture into each cup. Bake 15 minutes or just until set, but not browned. Cool. In small microwave-safe bowl, place chocolate chips and butter. Microwave at HIGH (100%) 30 seconds to 1 minute or until chips are melted and mixture is smooth when stirred. Drop teaspoonfuls of chocolate mixture onto center of each cheesecake, letting white show around edge. Place almond slices around chocolate mixture to resemble petals. Cover; refrigerate. About 2 dozen cheesecakes.

Simple Chocolate Cheesecakes

24 vanilla wafer cookies
2 packages (8 oz. each) cream
    cheese, softened
1¼ cups sugar
⅓ cup HERSHEY'S Cocoa
2 tablespoons all-purpose flour
3 eggs
1 cup (8 oz.) dairy sour cream
1 teaspoon vanilla extract
Sour Cream Topping
Canned cherry pie filling, chilled
Sour Cream Topping
    1 cup (8 oz.) dairy sour cream
    2 tablespoons sugar
    1 teaspoon vanilla extract

Heat oven to 325°F. Line muffin pans with foil laminated baking cups (2½ inches in diameter). Place one vanilla wafer on bottom of each cup. In large mixer bowl, beat cream cheese until smooth. Add sugar, cocoa and flour; blend well. Add eggs; beat well. Stir in sour cream and vanilla. Fill each prepared cup almost full with cheese mixture. Bake 20 to 25 minutes or until set. Remove from oven; cool 5 to 10 minutes. Spread heaping teaspoonful Sour Cream Topping on each cup. Cool completely in pans; refrigerate. Garnish with dollop of cherry pie filling just before serving. Refrigerate leftovers. About 2 dozen cheesecakes.

SOUR CREAM TOPPING: In small bowl, stir together sour cream, sugar and vanilla; stir until sugar dissolves.

Black-Eyed Susan Cheesecakes, Simple Chocolate Cheesecakes

German Chocolate Cheesecake

Coconut-Pecan Graham Crust
4 bars (4 oz.) HERSHEY'S Semi-
    Sweet Baking Chocolate,
    broken into pieces
3 packages (8 oz. each.) cream
    cheese, softened
¾ cup sugar
½ cup dairy sour cream
2 teaspoons vanilla extract
2 tablespoons all-purpose flour
3 eggs
Coconut Pecan Topping

Coconut-Pecan Graham Crust
    1 cup graham cracker crumbs
    2 tablespoons sugar
    ⅓ cup butter or margarine,
      melted
    ¼ cup flaked coconut
    ¼ cup chopped pecans

Coconut-Pecan Topping
    ½ cup (1 stick) butter or
      margarine
    ¼ cup packed light brown sugar
    2 tablespoons light cream
    2 tablespoons light corn syrup
    1 cup flaked coconut
    ½ cup chopped pecans
    1 teaspoon vanilla extract

Prepare Coconut-Pecan Graham Crust; set aside. Heat oven to 450°F. In small microwave-safe bowl, place chocolate. Microwave at HIGH (100%) 1 to 1½ minutes or until chocolate is melted and smooth when stirred; set aside. In large mixer bowl, combine cream cheese, sugar, sour cream and vanilla; beat on medium speed of electric mixer until smooth. Add flour, 1 tablespoon at a time, blending well. Add eggs and reserved chocolate; blend well. Pour into crust. Bake 10 minutes; without opening oven door, reduce oven temperature to 250°F. Continue baking 35 minutes; remove from oven. With knife, loosen cake from side of pan. Cool completely; remove rim of pan. Prepare Coconut-Pecan Topping. Spread topping over top of cake. Refrigerate until firm. 10 to 12 servings.

COCONUT-PECAN GRAHAM CRUST: Heat oven to 350°F. In small bowl, combine graham cracker crumbs and sugar. Stir in butter, coconut and pecans; mix thoroughly. Press mixture onto bottom and ½-inch up side of 9-inch springform pan. Bake 8 to 10 minutes. Cool.

COCONUT-PECAN TOPPING: In small saucepan, melt butter; add brown sugar, light cream and corn syrup. Cook over medium heat, stirring constantly, until smooth and bubbly. Remove from heat. Stir in coconut, pecans and vanilla. Cool slightly.

German Chocolate Cheesecake

Chocolate Pecan Cheesecake with Raspberry Sauce

¾ cup graham cracker crumbs

¾ cup pecan pieces, toasted
  and finely chopped*

¼ cup firmly packed brown sugar

½ cup (1 stick) butter or
  margarine, melted, divided

⅓ cup HERSHEY'S Cocoa

3 packages (8 oz. each) cream
  cheese, softened

1 can (14 oz.) sweetened
  condensed milk

4 eggs

1 tablespoon vanilla extract

Sweetened whipped cream

Additional pecans

Raspberry Sauce

Raspberry Sauce

  1 package (10 oz.) frozen red
    raspberries in light syrup,
    thawed

  ¼ cup red currant jelly or
    red raspberry jam

  1 tablespoon cornstarch

Heat oven to 350°F. In medium bowl, stir together graham cracker crumbs, pecans, brown sugar and ¼ cup butter. Press mixture firmly onto bottom of 9-inch springform pan. In small bowl, combine cocoa and remaining ¼ cup butter, stirring until smooth. In large mixer bowl, beat cream cheese until fluffy. Add cocoa mixture; mix well. Gradually add sweetened condensed milk, beating until smooth. Add eggs and vanilla; beat well. Pour batter over crust. Bake 1 hour or until set. Remove from oven to wire rack. With knife, loosen cake from side of pan. Cool completely; remove side of pan. Cover; refrigerate. Just before serving, top with whipped cream; garnish with additional pecans. Serve with Raspberry Sauce. Refrigerate leftovers. 10 to 12 servings.

RASPBERRY SAUCE: In small saucepan, combine raspberries, jelly and cornstarch. Cook over medium heat, stirring constantly, until thickened and clear. Cool. Refrigerate. About 1⅓ cups sauce.

* To toast pecans: Heat oven to 300° F. Spread pecans in thin layer in shallow baking pan. Bake 8 to 10 minutes, stirring occasionally, until crisp and light brown.

Vanilla Citrus Cheesecake with Chocolate Drizzle

Heat oven to 350°F. In small bowl, stir together crumbs, butter and 2 tablespoons sugar. Press mixture evenly onto bottom of 9-inch springform pan. Bake 5 minutes or just until golden brown; remove from oven (do *not* turn off oven). In large mixer bowl, beat cream cheese and remaining 1½ cups sugar until smooth. Add eggs, vanilla extract and orange peel; beat well. In small microwave-safe bowl, place vanilla milk chips. Microwave at HIGH (100%) 1 to 1½ minutes or until chips are melted and smooth when stirred vigorously. Blend into cream cheese mixture. Pour batter over crust. Bake 35 to 40 minutes or just until almost set. Remove from oven to wire rack. With knife, loosen cake from side of pan. Cool completely; remove side of pan. Cover; refrigerate until firm. Prepare Chocolate Drizzle; drop from spoon, shaking back and forth across cheesecake. 10 to 12 servings.

CHOCOLATE DRIZZLE: In small microwave-safe bowl, place chocolate chips and shortening. Microwave at HIGH (100%) 30 to 45 seconds or until chocolate is melted and mixture is smooth when stirred.

2 cups graham cracker crumbs
⅓ cup butter or margarine, melted
2 tablespoons plus 1½ cups sugar, divided
3 packages (8 oz. each) cream cheese, softened
4 eggs
1 teaspoon vanilla extract
1 teaspoon freshly grated orange peel
1⅔ cups (10-oz. pkg.) HERSHEY'S Vanilla Milk Chips
Chocolate Drizzle

Chocolate Drizzle
½ cup HERSHEY'S Semi-Sweet Chocolate Chips
1 tablespoon shortening

Chocolate Drizzled Peanut Butter Cheesecake

Graham Cracker Crust
3 packages (8 oz. each) cream
  cheese, softened
¾ cup sugar
1⅔ cups (10-oz. pkg.) REESE'S
  Peanut Butter Chips
¼ cup milk
4 eggs
1 teaspoon vanilla extract
Chocolate Drizzle

Graham Cracker Crust
  1 cup graham cracker crumbs
  3 tablespoons sugar
  3 tablespoons butter or
    margarine, melted

Chocolate Drizzle
  ½ cup HERSHEY'S Semi-
    Sweet Chocolate Chips
  1 tablespoon shortening

Prepare Graham Cracker Crust; set aside. Heat oven to 450°F. In large mixer bowl, beat cream cheese and sugar on medium speed of electric mixer until smooth. In small microwave-safe bowl, place peanut butter chips with milk. Microwave at HIGH (100%) 1 minute; stir. If necessary, microwave at HIGH an additional 15 seconds at a time, stirring after each heating, just until chips are melted when stirred. Blend peanut butter chip mixture into cream cheese mixture. Add eggs, one at a time, mixing well after each addition. Stir in vanilla. Pour batter over crust. Bake 10 minutes. Reduce oven temperature to 250°F.; continue baking 40 minutes. Remove from oven to wire rack. With knife, loosen cake from side of pan. Cool completely; remove side of pan. Prepare Chocolate Drizzle; drop from spoon, shaking back and forth across cheesecake. Cover; refrigerate. 10 to 12 servings.

GRAHAM CRACKER CRUST: Heat oven to 325°F. In small bowl, stir together graham cracker crumbs, sugar and butter. Press mixture evenly onto bottom of 9-inch springform pan. Bake 10 minutes. Remove from oven.

CHOCOLATE DRIZZLE: In small microwave-safe bowl, place chocolate chips and shortening. Microwave at HIGH (100%) 30 to 45 or until chocolate is melted and mixture is smooth when stirred.

Chocolate Drizzled Peanut Butter Cheesecake

Hershey Bar Cheesecake

Almond Crust
1 HERSHEY'S Milk Chocolate
   Bar (7 oz.), broken into pieces
4 packages (3 oz. each) cream
   cheese, softened
¾ cup sugar
2 tablespoons HERSHEY'S Cocoa
Dash salt
2 eggs
½ teaspoon vanilla extract
Sour Cream Topping

Almond Crust
   ¾ cup graham cracker
      crumbs
   ⅔ cup chopped slivered
      almonds
   2 tablespoons sugar
   ¼ cup (½ stick) butter or
      margarine, melted

Sour Cream Topping
   ½ cup dairy sour cream
   2 tablespoons sugar
   ½ teaspoon vanilla extract

Prepare Almond Crust; set aside. Heat oven to 325°F. In top of double boiler over hot, not boiling, water, melt chocolate bar pieces; set aside. In large mixer bowl, beat cream cheese until light and fluffy. Stir together sugar, cocoa and salt; blend into cream cheese mixture. Beat in eggs and vanilla. Add reserved melted chocolate; beat just until blended (do not overbeat). Pour batter into crust. Bake 35 to 40 minutes or until set. Remove from oven to wire rack. With knife, loosen cake from side of pan; cool to room temperature. Spread Sour Cream Topping over cheesecake, if desired. Refrigerate several hours or overnight; remove side of pan. Cover; refrigerate leftovers. 8 servings.

ALMOND CRUST: In medium bowl, stir together graham cracker crumbs, almonds and sugar. Stir in butter; blend well. Press mixture onto bottom and up side of 8-inch springform pan or round pan with removable bottom.

SOUR CREAM TOPPING: In small bowl, stir together sour cream, sugar and vanilla.

Celebration Cakes

Chocolate Lover's Torte

Chocolate Lover's Torte

Heat oven to 350°F. Generously grease and flour 2 heart-shaped or 9-inch round baking pans. In small saucepan, melt ¼ cup butter. Remove from heat; stir in cocoa. In large mixer bowl, beat ⅔ cup butter and 1 cup sugar until creamy. Add cocoa mixture, egg yolks, vanilla and almond extracts; beat until blended. Gradually add flour, salt and milk; beat until well blended. Stir in almonds. In small mixer bowl, beat egg whites until foamy; gradually add remaining 3 tablespoons sugar, beating just until soft peaks form. Gently fold into chocolate mixture. Pour batter into prepared pans. Bake 20 to 25 minutes or until wooden pick inserted in center comes out clean. Cool 10 minutes. (Cake will settle slightly.) Invert onto wire rack. Cool completely. Prepare Smooth and Glossy Chocolate Chip Glaze. Place one cake layer on serving plate; spoon half of glaze over layer. Top with second layer. Spread top and sides with remaining glaze. Cool until glaze is set. Garnish as desired. 10 to 12 servings.

SMOOTH AND GLOSSY CHOCOLATE CHIP GLAZE: In small saucepan, combine water and sugar. Heat to boiling, stirring until sugar is dissolved. Remove from heat; stir in chocolate chips and vanilla. Whisk or beat with spoon until well blended. Use immediately.

¼ cup (½ stick) butter
⅓ cup HERSHEY'S Cocoa
⅔ cup butter, softened
1 cup plus 3 tablespoons sugar, divided
3 eggs, separated
1 teaspoon vanilla extract
¼ teaspoon almond extract
¾ cup all-purpose flour
½ teaspoon salt
¼ cup milk
⅔ cup finely ground almonds
Sweetened whipped cream (optional)
Smooth and Glossy Chocolate Chip Glaze

Smooth and Glossy Chocolate Chip Glaze
 ¼ cup water
 3 tablespoons sugar
 1 cup HERSHEY'S MINI CHIPS Semi-Sweet Chocolate
 ½ teaspoon vanilla extract

Triple Chocolate Torte

Triple Chocolate Torte

Heat oven to 350°F. Grease and flour two 9-inch round baking pans or two heart-shaped pans. In small mixer bowl, beat egg whites until foamy; gradually add ½ cup sugar, beating until stiff peaks form. In large mixer bowl, stir together remaining 1 cup sugar, flour, cocoa, baking soda and salt. Add oil, buttermilk and egg yolks; beat until smooth. Gently fold egg whites into batter. Pour batter into prepared pans. Bake 25 to 30 minutes or until cake springs back when touched lightly in center. Cool 5 minutes; remove from pans to wire racks. Cool completely. Split layers in half horizontally. Prepare Chocolate Cream Filling. Spread cake layer with one-third filling; top with second cake layer. Repeat procedure ending with plain layer on top. Prepare Chocolate Glaze; glaze cake. Decorate with Chocolate Leaves, if desired. Refrigerate; store leftovers in refrigerator. 8 to 10 servings.

CHOCOLATE CREAM FILLING: In small mixer bowl, combine sugar and cocoa. Add cream and vanilla; beat on low speed of electric mixer to combine. Beat on medium speed until stiff. 3 cups filling.

CHOCOLATE GLAZE: In small saucepan, combine butter, corn syrup and water. Cook over medium heat, stirring constantly, until mixture begins to boil. Remove from heat; stir in chocolate chips until melted. Cool to room temperature. 1 cup glaze.

* To sour milk: Use 1 tablespoon white vinegar plus milk to equal 1 cup.

2 eggs, separated
1½ cups sugar, divided
1¼ cups all-purpose flour
½ cup HERSHEY'S Cocoa
¾ teaspoon baking soda
½ teaspoon salt
½ cup vegetable oil
1 cup buttermilk or sour milk
Chocolate Cream Filling
Chocolate Glaze
Chocolate leaves(see Garnishes page 121) or Chocolate Curls (Garnishes page 120 (optional))

Chocolate Cream Filling
⅔ cup sugar
⅓ cup HERSHEY'S Cocoa
1½ cups cold whipping cream
1½ teaspoons vanilla extract

Chocolate Glaze
3 tablespoons butter or margarine
3 tablespoons light corn syrup
1 tablespoon water
1 cup HERSHEY'S Semi-Sweet Chocolate Chips

Checkerboard Cake

¼ cup HERSHEY'S Cocoa
¼ cup boiling water
⅔ cup shortening
1¾ cups sugar
2 eggs
1 teaspoon vanilla extract
2¼ cups all-purpose flour
1½ teaspoons baking soda
½ teaspoon salt
1⅓ cups buttermilk or sour milk*
Cocoa Buttercream Frosting

Cocoa Buttercream Frosting
  2⅔ cups powdered sugar
  ½ cup HERSHEY'S Cocoa
  6 tablespoons butter or
    margarine, softened
  5 to 6 tablespoons milk
  1 teaspoon vanilla extract

Heat oven to 350°F. Grease and flour three 8-inch round baking pans. In small bowl, stir cocoa and water until smooth. Set aside. In large mixer bowl, beat shortening and sugar until light and fluffy. Add eggs and vanilla; beat well. Stir together flour, baking soda and salt; add alternately with buttermilk to shortening mixture, blending after each addition. Remove 2½ cups batter; set aside. Add cocoa mixture to remaining batter, blending well. Spoon ¾ cup white batter around outer edge of two prepared pans. Spoon ½ cup chocolate batter in a ring next to the inner edge of white batter in each of the pans. Spoon ¼ cup white batter into center of each pan. In third pan, spoon ¾ cup chocolate batter around outer edge of pan. Spoon ½ cup white batter to make inner ring. Fill center with ¼ cup chocolate batter. Bake 25 to 28 minutes or until wooden pick inserted in center comes out clean. Cool 10 minutes; remove from pans to wire racks. Cool completely. Frost with Cocoa Buttercream Frosting, stacking cake layers so outside colors alternate. (Use very thin layer of frosting between cake layers so checkerboard effect will not be destroyed.)

COCOA BUTTERCREAM FROSTING: Stir together powdered sugar and cocoa. In small mixer bowl, beat butter with ½ cup cocoa mixture until well blended. Add remaining cocoa mixture alternately with milk and vanilla, beating to spreading consistency. About 2 cups frosting.

* To sour milk: Use 4 teaspoons white vinegar plus milk to equal 1⅓ cups.

Luscious Filled Chocolate Gems

Heat oven to 350°F. Paper-line small muffin cups (1¾ inches in diameter). In small mixer bowl, beat butter, granulated sugar and vanilla until creamy. Add egg; beat well. Stir together flour, cocoa, baking soda and salt; add to butter mixture alternately with buttermilk. Beat until well blended. Add water; blend well. Spoon about 2 teaspoons batter into each prepared cup. Bake 10 to 12 minutes or until wooden pick inserted in center comes out clean. Cool thoroughly. Sift powdered sugar on top of cupcakes. Spoon Chocolate Cream Filling into pastry bag fitted with small star tip. Insert tip into center of cupcake, releasing about 1½ teaspoons filling inside and on top of each. Refrigerate until filling is set. Garnish with orange peel, if desired. About 4 dozen small cupcakes.

CHOCOLATE CREAM FILLING: In small saucepan over low heat, melt butter. Add cocoa and granulated sugar; stir until well blended. Remove from heat; cool. In small mixer bowl, beat cream cheese and vanilla until smooth. Add cocoa mixture; beat well. Add powdered sugar; beat until blended. Stir in orange peel, if desired. About 1½ cups filling.

* To sour milk: Use ¾ teaspoon white vinegar plus milk to equal ¼ cup.

6 tablespoons butter or
  margarine, softened
¾ cup granulated sugar
¾ teaspoon vanilla extract
1 egg
1 cup all-purpose flour
¼ cup HERSHEY'S Cocoa
½ teaspoon baking soda
⅛ teaspoon salt
¼ cup buttermilk or sour milk*
¼ cup boiling water
Powdered sugar
Chocolate Cream Filling
Freshly grated orange peel
  (optional)

Chocolate Cream Filling
  ¼ cup (½ stick) butter
    or margarine
  ⅓ cup HERSHEY'S Cocoa
  ⅓ cup granulated sugar
  2 packages (3 oz. each) cream
    cheese, softened
  1 teaspoon vanilla extract
  ½ cup powdered sugar
  ½ teaspoon freshly grated
    orange peel (optional)

Black Magic Cake

Black Magic Cake

Heat oven to 350°F. Grease and flour one 13 x 9 x 2-inch baking pan. In large mixer bowl, stir together sugar, flour, cocoa, baking soda, baking powder and salt. Add eggs, coffee, buttermilk, oil and vanilla; beat on medium speed of electric mixer 2 minutes (batter will be thin). Pour batter into prepared pan. Bake 35 to 40 minutes or until wooden pick inserted in center comes out clean. Cool completely in pan on wire rack. Frost as desired. Garnish with green tinted coconut and jelly beans, if desired. 12 servings.

* To sour milk: Use 1 tablespoon white vinegar plus milk to equal 1 cup.

2 cups sugar

1¾ cups all-purpose flour

¾ cup HERSHEY'S Cocoa

2 teaspoons baking soda

1 teaspoon baking powder

1 teaspoon salt

2 eggs

1 cup strong black coffee or 2 teaspoons powdered instant coffee plus 1 cup boiling water

1 cup buttermilk or sour milk*

½ cup vegetable oil

1 teaspoon vanilla extract

Flaked coconut (optional)

Jelly beans (optional)

Coconut may be tinted by combining 1 teaspoon water with a few drops of liquid food color in a tightly covered jar. Add desired amount of coconut, cover and shake until evenly tinted.

BAKER'S HINT

California Strawberry Log

California Strawberry Log

Heat oven to 375°F. Line 15½ x 10½ x 1-inch jelly roll pan with foil; generously grease foil. In large mixer bowl, beat egg yolks on high speed of electric mixer 3 minutes. Gradually add ½ cup granulated sugar; continue beating 2 minutes. Stir together flour, cocoa, ⅓ cup granulated sugar, baking soda and salt; add alternately with water and vanilla to egg yolk mixture, beating on low speed just until smooth. In small mixer bowl, beat egg whites until foamy. Add 1 tablespoon granulated sugar and beat until stiff peaks form; carefully fold into chocolate mixture. Spread batter evenly into prepared pan. Bake 15 to 18 minutes or until top springs back when touched lightly. Invert on towel sprinkled with 2 tablespoons powdered sugar; carefully remove foil. Immediately roll cake and towel together from narrow end; place on wire rack to cool. In clean large mixer bowl, beat whipping cream, remaining ¾ cup powdered sugar and vanilla on high speed of electric mixer until stiff. Fold sliced strawberries into 2 cups of the whipped cream; reserve remaining whipped cream for garnish. Unroll cake and spread with strawberry-cream mixture. Reroll. Garnish with reserved whipped cream and chopped strawberries, if desired. Refrigerate 1 hour or longer before serving. Refrigerate leftovers. 8 to 10 servings.

3 eggs, separated
½ cup granulated sugar
½ cup all-purpose flour
⅓ cup HERSHEY'S Cocoa
⅓ cup granulated sugar
½ teaspoon baking soda
¼ teaspoon salt
⅓ cup water
1 teaspoon vanilla extract
1 tablespoon granulated sugar
2 tablespoons plus ¾ cup powdered sugar, divided
2 cups (1 pt.) cold whipping cream
1 teaspoon vanilla extract
3 cups sliced fresh strawberries or two packages (16 oz. each) frozen strawberries
Additional strawberries, coarsely chopped (optional)

Chocolate Petits Fours

4 eggs, separated

¾ cup sugar, divided

¾ cup ground blanched almonds

⅓ cup all-purpose flour

⅓ cup HERSHEY'S Cocoa

½ teaspoon baking soda

¼ teaspoon salt

¼ cup water

1 teaspoon vanilla extract

¼ teaspoon almond extract

Raspberry or apricot preserves

Milk Chocolate Glaze or
    Semi-Sweet Chocolate Glaze

Assorted decorating gel or
    decorating frosting

Heat oven to 375°F. Line 15½ x 10½ x 1-inch jelly roll pan with foil; generously grease foil. In small mixer bowl, beat egg yolks on medium speed of electric mixer 3 minutes. Gradually add ½ cup sugar; continue beating 2 additional minutes. In separate bowl, stir together almonds, flour, cocoa, baking soda and salt; add to egg yolk mixture alternately with water, vanilla and almond extract, beating just until batter is smooth. In large mixer bowl, with clean beaters, beat egg whites until soft peaks form; gradually add remaining ¼ cup sugar; continue beating until stiff peaks form. Gradually fold chocolate mixture into beaten egg whites until well blended. Spread batter evenly into prepared pan. Bake 16 to 18 minutes or until top springs back when touched lightly. Immediately loosen cake from edges of pan; invert onto large wire rack. Carefully peel off foil. Turn right side up; cool completely.

To prepare Petits Fours: Cut cake into hearts, diamonds, circles or squares with small cookie cutters (approximately 1½-inch shapes). Sandwich similar shapes together with thin layer of raspberry or apricot preserves. Place petits fours on wire rack with wax-paper-covered cookie sheet below to catch drips. Cover until ready to glaze. Prepare either Milk Chocolate Glaze or Semi-Sweet Chocolate Glaze. Frost by spooning glaze over cake pieces until entire piece is covered. (Glaze that drips off can be reheated and used again.) Allow glaze to set. Refrigerate, if necessary. Pipe decorations with glossy decorating gel or tinted frostings. Cover; store in cool place (will keep several days). About 2 dozen petits fours.

MILK CHOCOLATE GLAZE: In small microwave-safe bowl, place chocolate pieces and shortening. Microwave at HIGH (100%) 45 seconds or until chocolate is melted and mixture is smooth when stirred. Cool slightly before using, stirring occasionally.

SEMI-SWEET CHOCOLATE GLAZE: In small microwave-safe bowl, place chocolate chips, butter and oil. Microwave at HIGH (100%) 1 minute or until chocolate is melted and mixture is smooth when stirred. If neccessary, microwave at HIGH an additional 15 seconds at a time, stirring after each heating. Cool slightly before using, stirring occasionally.

Milk Chocolate Glaze
  1 HERSHEY'S Milk Chocolate Bar (7 oz.), broken into pieces
  2 tablespoons shortening (do not use butter or oil)

Semi-Sweet Chocolate Glaze
  1 cup HERSHEY'S Semi-Sweet Chocolate Chips
  ¼ cup unsalted butter
  2 teaspoons vegetable oil

Chocolate Raspberry Pound Cake

Chocolate Raspberry Pound Cake

Heat oven to 350°F. Grease and flour 12-cup fluted tube pan. In small microwave-safe bowl, place ¾ cup preserves. Microwave at HIGH (100%) 30 to 45 seconds or until melted; cool. In large mixer bowl, stir together flour, granulated sugar, cocoa, baking soda and salt. Add butter, sour cream, eggs, vanilla and melted preserves; beat on medium speed of electric mixer 3 to 4 minutes until well blended. Pour batter into prepared pan. Bake 50 to 60 minutes or until wooden pick inserted in center comes out clean. Cool 10 minutes; remove from pan to wire rack. In small microwave-safe bowl, place remaining ¼ cup preserves. Microwave at HIGH 30 seconds or until melted; brush over warm cake. Cool completely. At serving time, sprinkle powdered sugar over top. Fill cake cavity with Raspberry Cream. About 12 servings.

RASPBERRY CREAM: Puree raspberries in food processor or blender. In medium bowl, strain to remove seeds; discard seeds. Blend topping with raspberry puree. Stir in liqueur, if desired.

* Red raspberry jam may be substituted.

1 cup seedless black raspberry
  preserves, divided*
2 cups all-purpose flour
1½ cups granulated sugar
¾ cup HERSHEY'S Cocoa
1½ teaspoons baking soda
1 teaspoon salt
⅔ cup butter or margarine,
  softened
2 cups (16 oz.) dairy sour cream
2 eggs
1 teaspoon vanilla extract
Powdered sugar
Raspberry Cream

Raspberry Cream
  1 package (10 oz.) frozen red
    raspberries in light
    syrup, thawed
  3½ cups (8 oz.) frozen non-
    dairy whipped topping,
    thawed
  2 tablespoons raspberry
    flavored liqueur (optional)

Hershey's Chocolate Almond Wedding Cake

Hershey's Chocolate Almond Wedding Cake

Prepare Chocolate Almond Brownie Layers and Almond Cake Layers. Prepare Frostings; keep covered with damp cloth until ready to use. To assemble tiers; spread each brownie layer with Creamy Buttercream Frosting; top with matching size almond layer. To assemble cake, place largest cake tiers on large serving platter. Frost with Creamy Buttercream Frosting. Place second largest tiers on first tier; frost with Creamy Buttercream Frosting. Place smallest tier on top of 8-inch separator plate set; frost with buttercream frosting. Place One-Bowl Buttercream Frosting in pastry bag fitted with large shell tip. Pipe frosting along edge of each cake tier. Garnish with Chocolate Filigree Hearts, if desired. Just before serving, place separator plate bottom on top of 10-inch cake tier. Fit with columns; add flowers, if desired. Place top tier on columns. Place flowers on top of cake, if desired. About 100 servings.

CHOCOLATE ALMOND BROWNIE LAYERS (prepare 2 recipes): Heat oven to 350°F. Grease well and flour 12 x 2-inch, 10 x 2-inch and 6 x 2-inch round baking pans. In microwave-safe bowl, place chocolate. Microwave at HIGH (100%) 2½ to 3 minutes or until melted when stirred. In large bowl of heavy duty mixer, beat butter and 3½ cups sugar until fluffy. Add egg yolks, beating well after each addition; add chocolate. Blend in flour, almonds and almond extract. In clean separate bowl, beat egg whites until foamy. Beat in cream of tartar and remaining ¼ cup sugar; beat until stiff but not dry. Fold egg whites into chocolate batter. Pour batter into prepared 12-inch pan. Bake 25 to 30 minutes or until wooden pick inserted 1½ inches from edge of pan comes out clean, center of cake will be slightly underdone. Repeat preparation of batter. Pour 2½ cups batter into prepared 6-inch pan; pour remaining batter into prepared 10-inch pan. Bake 20 to 30 minutes or until

12, 10, and 6-inch Chocolate
    Almond Brownie Layers
12, 10, and 6-inch Almond
    Cake Layers
Creamy Buttercream Frosting
One-Bowl Buttercream Frosting
Chocolate Filigree Hearts (See
    Garnishes, page 120)

12,10 and 6-inch Chocolate Almond
Brownie Layers
    5 bars (5 oz.) HERSHEY'S
        Unsweetened Baking
        Chocolate
    1½ cups (3 sticks) butter or
        margarine
    3¾ cups sugar, divided
    8 eggs, separated
    2½ cups all-purpose flour
    1½ cups very finely ground
        blanched almonds
    1 teaspoon almond extract
    ½ teaspoon cream of tartar

12,10 and 6-inch Almond Cake Layers

  3 cups (6 sticks) butter or margarine

  1¾ cups granulated sugar

  8 eggs

  2 cups all-purpose flour

  2 cups finely ground blanched almonds

  2¼ teaspoons baking powder

  ⅔ cup milk

  2 teaspoons almond extract

Creamy Buttercream Frosting

  1 cup (2 sticks) butter or margarine, softened

  1 cup butter-flavor shortening

  2 teaspoons vanilla extract

  7½ cups powdered sugar

  4 tablespoons milk

One-Bowl Buttercream Frosting

  6 tablespoons butter or margarine, softened

  2⅔ cups powdered sugar

  ½ cup HERSHEY'S Cocoa

  4 to 6 tablespoons milk

  1 teaspoon vanilla extract

done. Cool layers 10 minutes; remove from pans to wire racks. Cool completely.

ALMOND CAKE LAYERS (prepare 2 recipes): Heat oven to 325°F. Grease well and flour 12 x 2-inch, 10 x 2-inch and 6 x 2-inch round baking pans. In large bowl of heavy duty mixer, beat butter and sugar until fluffy. Add eggs; beat well. Stir together dry ingredients; add alternately with milk to egg mixture. Add almond extract. Pour batter into prepared 12-inch pan. Bake 50 minutes or until wooden pick inserted in center comes out clean. Repeat preparation of batter. Pour 2½ cups batter into prepared 6-inch pan; pour remaining batter into prepared 10-inch pan. Bake both layers 40 to 45 minutes or until wooden pick inserted in center comes out clean. Cool layers 10 minutes; remove from pans to wire racks. Cool completely.

CREAMY BUTTERCREAM FROSTING (prepare 2 recipes): In large bowl of heavy duty mixer, beat butter and shortening until blended; blend in vanilla. Gradually add powdered sugar, alternately with milk until well blended. Beat on high speed until fluffy. About 5½ cups frosting.

ONE-BOWL BUTTERCREAM FROSTING: In small mixer bowl, beat butter. Add powdered sugar and cocoa alternately with milk; beat to spreading consistency. Blend in vanilla. About 2 cups frosting.

Fantasy Fruit and Cream Filled Chocolate Shortcake

Heat oven to 400°F. Prepare Creamy Filling, refrigerate. Line 8-inch square baking pan with foil; butter foil. In medium bowl, stir together baking mix, sugar and cocoa. Stir in milk, butter and vanilla. Mix just until all dry ingredients are moistened. Spread batter evenly in prepared pan. Bake 20 to 25 minutes or until wooden pick inserted in center comes out clean. Cool 15 minutes; carefully remove shortcake from pan. (Shortcake may be served warm or completely cooled.)

Cut shortcake into 9 squares; split each square horizontally in half. On serving plates, fill each shortcake with about ⅓ cup filling and fruit. Top with dollop of filling. Garnish with whole strawberry. Serve with syrup drizzled over top. 9 servings.

CREAMY FILLING: In small mixer bowl, combine whipping cream, powdered sugar and vanilla. Beat on high speed of electric mixer until stiff. Beat in sour cream. Filling may be refrigerated up to 2 hours before serving.

* Fresh oranges, peeled and cut into sections, or canned mandarin orange segments can be substituted.

Creamy Filling
2¼ cups all-purpose biscuit
    baking mix
⅓ cup sugar
⅓ cup HERSHEY'S Cocoa
¾ cup milk
¼ cup (½ stick) butter or
    margarine, melted
1 teaspoon vanilla extract
2 cups sliced fresh or frozen
    strawberries
1 cup sliced kiwi fruit
9 whole fresh strawberries
HERSHEY'S Syrup

Creamy Filling
    1½ cups cold whipping cream
    3 tablespoons powdered sugar
    ¾ teaspoon vanilla extract
    ¾ cup dairy sour cream

Chocolate Chip Berry Shortcake

2 cups all-purpose biscuit
   baking mix
⅓ cup sugar
1 egg
½ cup milk
2 tablespoons vegetable oil
½ cup HERSHEY'S MINI
   CHIPS Semi-Sweet Chocolate
Sweetened whipped cream
4 cups (1 qt.) strawberries, sliced
   and sweetened

Heat oven to 375°F. Grease 8-inch round baking pan. In medium bowl, stir together baking mix and sugar. In second bowl, slightly beat egg; blend in milk and oil. Add to dry ingredients; stir just until moistened (batter may be lumpy). Stir in small chocolate chips. Spoon batter into prepared pan. Bake 25 to 30 minutes or until wooden pick inserted in center comes out clean. Cool 10 minutes; remove from pan. Place on serving plate. Cut into wedges; top with sweetened whipped cream and strawberries. 8 servings.

Chocolate Chip Berry Shortcake

Independence Day Chocolate Cake

Independence Day Chocolate Cake

Heat oven to 350°F. Grease and flour 15½ x 10½ x 1-inch jelly roll pan. In small bowl, combine cocoa and water; stir until smooth. Set aside. In small mixer bowl, beat shortening, sugar, vanilla and egg. Stir together flour, baking soda and salt; add alternately with buttermilk to shortening mixture. Stir in cocoa mixture. Spread batter into prepared pan. Bake 28 to 30 minutes or until wooden pick inserted in center comes out clean. Cool in pan on wire rack. Prepare Vanilla Frosting. Remove about ¾ cup ; add food color to ½ cup frosting to tint desired shade of blue. Set aside the blue and ¼ cup Vanilla Frosting. Spread reserved Vanilla Frosting over top of cake. Spread blue frosting in upper left corner. Pipe stars on blue with remaining Vanilla Frosting. Shortly before serving, place strawberries in seven rows to represent red stripes of flag. About 15 servings.

VANILLA FROSTING: In large mixer bowl, beat butter until creamy. Gradually add 2 cups powdered sugar, beating well. Slowly add milk and vanilla, beating until well blended. Gradually add remaining 4 cups powdered sugar, beating to spreading consistency. Add additional milk, if needed, for thinner consistency. About 3 cups frosting.

* To sour milk: Use 4 teaspoons white vinegar plus milk to equal 1⅓ cups.

½ cup HERSHEY'S Cocoa
½ cup boiling water
⅔ cup shortening
1½ cups sugar
1 teaspoon vanilla extract
2 eggs
2 cups all-purpose flour
1½ teaspoons baking soda
½ teaspoon salt
1⅓ cups buttermilk or sour milk*
Vanilla Frosting
Blue food color
2 cups (1 pt.) fresh strawberries, cut into pieces

Vanilla Frosting
  ½ cup (1 stick) butter or margarine, softened
  6 cups powdered sugar, divided
  6 tablespoons milk
  2¼ teaspoons vanilla extract

Supreme Chocolate Almond Torte

3 eggs

1¼ cups sugar

1 cup (2 sticks) butter or
  margarine, melted

1 teaspoon vanilla extract

Dash salt

½ cup HERSHEY'S Premium
  European Style Cocoa

⅓ cup all-purpose flour

¾ cup toasted almonds, very
  finely chopped

Supreme Cocoa Glaze

Supreme Cocoa Glaze

  2 tablespoons butter or
    margarine

  2 tablespoons HERSHEY'S
    Premium European Style
    Cocoa

  2 tablespoons water

  1 cup powdered sugar

  ½ teaspoon vanilla extract

Heat oven to 350°F. Line 9-inch round baking pan with foil; butter bottom only. In large mixer bowl, beat eggs, sugar, butter, vanilla and salt; beat on high speed of electric mixer 3 minutes until smooth and thick, scraping bowl often. Add cocoa and flour; blend well. Stir in almonds. Spread batter into prepared pan. Bake 35 to 40 minutes or until wooden pick inserted in center comes out clean. Cool on wire rack 15 minutes; remove from pan. Carefully peel off foil; cool completely. Place on serving plate. Spread Supreme Cocoa Glaze over top and sides; garnish with sliced almonds, if desired. 10 to 12 servings.

SUPREME COCOA GLAZE: In small saucepan over low heat, melt butter; add cocoa and water, stirring constantly until mixture thickens. Do not boil. Remove from heat; gradually add powdered sugar and vanilla, beating with spoon until smooth. Add additional water, ½ teaspoon at a time, until desired consistency. About ¾ cup glaze.

Supreme Chocolate Almond Torte

Chocolate Ice Cream Cake

2 eggs, separated
1½ cups sugar, divided
1¼ cups all-purpose flour
½ cup HERSHEY'S Cocoa
¾ teaspoon baking soda
½ teaspoon salt
½ cup vegetable oil
1 cup buttermilk or sour milk*
Ice Cream Layers
¾ cup sweetened whipped cream
  or non-dairy whipped topping
½ cup sweetened fresh fruit
Chocolate Cream Rosettes (see
  Garnishes, page 119)

Ice Cream Layers
  ½ gallon ice cream, any flavor,
  slightly softened

Heat oven to 350°F. Grease and flour three 9-inch round baking pans (if only 2 pans are available, reserve ⅓ of the batter in refrigerator while the first 2 layers are baking.) In small mixer bowl, beat egg whites until foamy; gradually beat in ½ cup sugar until stiff peaks form. Set aside. In large mixer bowl, stir together flour, remaining 1 cup sugar, cocoa, baking soda and salt. Add oil, buttermilk and egg yolks; beat until smooth. Gently fold egg white mixture into batter. Pour about 1⅔ cups batter into each prepared pan. Bake 18 to 20 minutes or until cake springs back when touched lightly in center. Cool 5 minutes; remove from pans to wire racks. (Bake remaining layer, if necessary.) Cool completely. Wrap each layer separately in foil; freeze several hours or several days in advance of serving. Prepare ice cream layers. Remove cake and ice cream layers from freezer; peel off foil. On serving plate, alternately layer cake and ice cream layers beginning and ending with cake. Wrap tightly; return to freezer. Just before serving, frost top.of cake with whipped cream. Arrange fruit slices in decorative design; pipe on Chocolate Cream Rosettes, if desired. About 10 servings.

ICE CREAM LAYERS: Line two 9-inch round layer pans with foil; working quickly, evenly spread your favorite flavor ice cream about ¾ inch deep in pans. Cover tightly; freeze until firm.

* To sour milk: Use 1 tablespoon white vinegar plus milk to equal 1 cup.

Chocolate Ice Cream Cake

Italian Ricotta Torte

8 eggs, separated
1½ cups sugar, divided
1½ cups finely ground blanched
   almonds
⅔ cup all-purpose flour
⅔ cup HERSHEY'S Cocoa
1 teaspoon baking soda
½ teaspoon salt
½ cup water
2 teaspoons vanilla extract
½ teaspoon almond extract
Ricotta Cherry Filling
Cocoa Whipped Cream Frosting

Ricotta Cherry Filling
   1 cup (½ pt.) cold whipping
     cream
   1¾ cups (15-oz. container)
     ricotta cheese
   ⅓ cup powdered sugar
   ½ cup chopped candied cherries
   ½ teaspoon almond extract

Cocoa Whipped Cream Frosting
   ⅔ cup powdered sugar
   ⅓ cup HERSHEY'S Cocoa
   2 cups (1 pt.) cold
     whipping cream
   2 teaspoons vanilla extract

Heat oven to 375°F. Grease and paper line two 9-inch round baking pans. In large mixer bowl, beat egg yolks on medium speed of electric mixer 3 minutes. Gradually add 1 cup sugar, beating 2 minutes. Stir together almonds, flour, cocoa, baking soda and salt; add alternately with water to egg yolk mixture, beating on low speed of mixer just until blended. Stir in vanilla and almond extracts. In large mixer bowl, beat egg whites until foamy. Gradually add remaining ½ cup sugar, beating until stiff peaks form. Carefully fold chocolate mixture into beaten egg whites. Spread batter evenly into prepared pans. Bake 20 to 22 minutes or until top springs back when touched lightly. Cool 10 minutes; remove from pans to wire racks. Cool completely. With long serrated knife, cut each layer in half horizontally. Refrigerate layers while preparing filling and frosting. Place one cake layer on serving plate; spread with about 1⅓ cups Ricotta Cherry Filling. Top with another cake layer. Repeat with remaining filling and cake layers. Frost sides and top of torte with Cocoa Whipped Cream Frosting. Garnish as desired. Refrigerate at least 4 hours. Refrigerate leftovers. 8 to 10 servings.

RICOTTA CHERRY FILLING: In small mixer bowl, beat whipping cream until stiff. In large mixer bowl, beat ricotta cheese and powdered sugar until smooth. Fold whipped cream into cheese mixture just until blended. Stir in candied cherries and almond extract. About 4 cups filling.

COCOA WHIPPED CREAM FROSTING: In large mixer bowl, stir together powdered sugar and cocoa. Blend in whipping cream and vanilla; beat until stiff. About 4 cups frosting.

Dandy Cake

Heat oven to 350°F. Grease and flour 15½ x 10½ x 1 inch jelly roll pan. In small saucepan, combine water, butter and cocoa. Cook over medium heat, stirring constantly, until mixture boils; boil and stir 1 minute. Remove from heat; set aside. In large mixer bowl, stir together flour, sugar, baking soda and salt. Add eggs and sour cream; blend well. Add chocolate mixture; beat just until blended (batter will be thin). Pour batter into prepared pan. Bake 25 to 30 minutes or until wooden pick inserted in center comes out clean. Do not remove cake from pan; spread peanut butter over warm cake. Cool completely in pan on wire rack. Prepare Chocolate Topping; carefully spread over top, covering peanut butter. Allow topping to set; cut into squares. About 15 servings.

CHOCOLATE TOPPING: In small saucepan over low heat, combine chocolate chips and shortening; stir until melted.

1 cup water
1 cup (2 sticks) butter or
  margarine
⅓ cup HERSHEY'S Cocoa
2 cups all-purpose flour
2 cups sugar
1 teaspoon baking soda
½ teaspoon salt
3 eggs
¾ cup dairy sour cream
¾ cup REESE'S Creamy
  Peanut Butter
Chocolate Topping

Chocolate Topping
  2 cups (12-oz. pkg.)
    HERSHEY'S Semi-Sweet
    Chocolate Chips
  2 tablespoons shortening

A wet utensil or the condensation of steam droplets can cause chocolate to get stiff and grainy. If this happens stir in 1 teaspoon solid vegetable shortening (not butter) for every 2 ounces chocolate.

BAKER'S HINT

Halloween Chocolate Cake

Halloween Chocolate Cake

Heat oven to 350°F. Grease and flour 12-cup fluted tube pan. In bowl, stir together chocolate bar pieces, butter and boiling water until chocolate is melted. In large mixer bowl, stir together flour, sugar, cocoa, baking soda and salt; gradually add butter mixture, beating until thoroughly blended. On medium speed, blend in eggs, sour cream and vanilla; beat 1 minute. Pour batter into prepared pan. Bake 50 to 55 minutes or until wooden pick inserted in center of cake comes out clean. Cool 10 minutes; remove from pan to wire rack. Cool completely. Drizzle Orange Frosting over cake. Place Chocolate Coated Ice Cream Cone into center of cake for pumpkin stem. Using leaf decorator tip, pipe leaves onto pumpkin with Decorator Frosting. 10 to 12 servings.

ORANGE FROSTING: In microwave-safe bowl, place butter. Microwave at HIGH (100%) 1 minute or until melted. Stir in powdered sugar, orange peel and vanilla. Stir in water for desired frosting consistency. Blend in food color for desired color.

DECORATOR FROSTING: In small mixer bowl, combine water and meringue powder. Add powdered sugar and vanilla; beat on high speed of electric mixer until stiff. Blend in green food color for desired color.

1 HERSHEY'S Milk Chocolate
  Bar (7 oz.), broken into pieces
½ cup (1 stick) butter or margarine
1 cup boiling water
2 cups all-purpose flour
1½ cups sugar
½ cup HERSHEY'S Cocoa
2 teaspoons baking soda
1 teaspoon salt
2 eggs
½ cup dairy sour cream
1 teaspoon vanilla extract
Chocolate Coated Ice Cream Cone
  (see Garnishes, page 121)
Orange Frosting
Decorator Frosting

Orange Frosting
  ⅓ cup butter or margarine
  2 cups powdered sugar
  2 teaspoons grated orange peel
  1½ teaspoons vanilla extract
  2 to 4 teaspoons hot water
  Red and yellow food color

Decorator Frosting
  3 tablespoons water
  1 tablespoon meringue powder
  1¼ to 1½ cups powdered sugar
  ⅛ teaspoon vanilla
  Green food color

Mini Chips Swirl Rum Cake

1 cup (2 sticks) butter or
   margarine, softened
2 cups sugar
1½ teaspoons vanilla extract
3 eggs
3 cups all-purpose flour
2 teaspoons baking powder
½ teaspoon salt
1 cup milk
¾ cup HERSHEY'S MINI
   CHIPS Semi-Sweet Chocolate
½ cup finely chopped nuts
Butter Rum Syrup
Chocolate Glaze

Butter Rum Syrup
   ½ cup sugar
   2 tablespoons butter
   2 tablespoons water
   ¼ cup rum or 1 teaspoon rum
      extract plus water to equal
      ¼ cup

Chocolate Glaze
   ¼ cup water
   3 tablespoons sugar
   1 cup HERSHEY'S MINI
      CHIPS Semi-Sweet Chocolate
   ½ teaspoon vanilla extract

Heat oven to 350°F. Grease and flour 10-inch tube pan or 12-cup fluted tube pan. In large mixer bowl, beat butter, sugar and vanilla until light and fluffy. Add eggs, one at a time, beating well after each addition. Stir together flour, baking powder and salt; add alternately with milk to butter mixture, beating until smooth. Remove 2 cups batter; set aside. Pour remaining batter into prepared pan. In small bowl, stir together small chocolate chips and nuts; sprinkle evenly over batter in pan. Spoon reserved batter over chip-nut mixture; carefully spread with spatula to cover. Bake 1 hour and 5 to 15 minutes or until wooden pick inserted in center of cake comes out clean. Cool 10 minutes; remove from pan to wire rack. Prepare Butter Rum Syrup. With fork, carefully pierce top and sides of warm cake. Gradually spoon or brush syrup onto cake. Allow syrup to dry and cake cool completely. Glaze with Chocolate Glaze. 12 to 16 servings.

BUTTER RUM SYRUP: In small saucepan, stir together sugar, butter and water. Cook over medium heat, stirring occasionally, until mixture comes to full rolling boil; boil 2 minutes. Remove from heat; stir in rum.

CHOCOLATE GLAZE: In small saucepan, combine water and sugar. Cook over low heat, stirring constantly, until mixture boils and sugar is dissolved. Remove from heat; stir in small chocolate chips and vanilla. Beat with spoon or wire whisk until well blended. Cool 5 minutes or to spreading consistency. Use immediately.

Mini Chips Swirl Rum Cake

Chocolate Raspberry Torte

1⅓ cups all-purpose flour

1 cup sugar, divided

1½ teaspoons baking powder

½ teaspoon salt

2 eggs, separated

1 cup (½ pt.) cold whipping
  cream

½ teaspoon almond extract

Chocolate Filling & Frosting

½ cup sliced almonds

¼ cup seedless raspberry
  preserves

½ cup sweetened whipped
  cream (optional)

Chocolate Filling & Frosting

  ⅔ cup sugar

  ⅓ cup HERSHEY'S Cocoa

  1½ cups cold whipping cream

  1½ teaspoons vanilla extract

Heat oven to 350°F. Grease and flour two 8 or 9-inch round baking pans. Stir together flour, ½ cup sugar, baking powder and salt. In large mixer bowl, beat egg whites until foamy; gradually add ¼ cup sugar, beating until stiff peaks form. In small mixer bowl, beat whipping cream until stiff; fold into beaten egg whites. In clean small mixer bowl, combine egg yolks, remaining ¼ cup sugar and almond extract; beat on medium speed of electric mixer 3 minutes until thick and lemon colored. Gently fold into whipped cream mixture. Gradually fold flour mixture into whipped cream mixture, just until ingredients are blended (mixture will be thick). Divide batter evenly between prepared pans; smooth surface. Bake 25 to 30 minutes or until cake springs back when touched lightly in center. Cool 5 minutes; remove from pans to wire rack. Cool completely. Prepare Chocolate Filling & Frosting. Split each cake layer in half horizontally. Place one layer on serving plate; spread with Chocolate Filling. Sprinkle with 1 tablespoon almonds; repeat with two more layers. Top with last layer, spread with raspberry preserves. Frost sides of cake with remaining Chocolate Filling. Garnish top edge with whipped cream, if desired. Sprinkle edge and center with remaining almonds; refrigerate until ready to serve. 16 servings.

CHOCOLATE FILLING & FROSTING: In small mixer bowl, stir together sugar and cocoa. Add whipping cream and vanilla, beat until stiff. About 3 cups filling and frosting.

Chocolate Raspberry Torte, Chocolate and Vanilla Yule Log

Chocolate and Vanilla Yule Log

4 eggs, separated
½ cup plus ⅓ cup sugar, divided
1 teaspoon vanilla extract
½ cup all-purpose flour
¼ cup HERSHEY'S Cocoa or
   HERSHEY'S Premium
   European Style Cocoa
½ teaspoon baking powder
¼ teaspoon baking soda
⅛ teaspoon salt
⅓ cup water
Vanilla Cream Filling
Chocolate Glaze
Vanilla Leaves (see Garnishes,
   page 121)
Candied cherries (optional)

Vanilla Cream Filling
   ½ teaspoon unflavored gelatin
   1 tablespoon cold water
   ⅔ cup HERSHEY'S Vanilla
      Milk Chips
   ¼ cup milk
   1 teaspoon vanilla extract
   1 cup (½ pt.) cold
      whipping cream

Heat oven to 375°F. Line 15½ x 10½ x 1-inch jelly roll pan with foil; generously grease foil. In large mixer bowl, beat egg whites until soft peaks form; gradually add ½ cup sugar, beating until stiff peaks form. Set aside. In small mixer bowl, beat egg yolks and vanilla on high speed of electric mixer about 3 minutes; gradually add remaining ⅓ cup sugar. Continue beating 2 additional minutes or until mixture is thick and lemon colored. In separate bowl, stir together flour, cocoa, baking powder, baking soda and salt; gently fold into egg yolk mixture alternately with water just until mixture is smooth. Gradually fold chocolate mixture into egg whites; spread evenly into prepared pan. Bake 12 to 15 minutes or until top springs back when touched lightly in center. Immediately loosen cake from edges of pan; invert on towel sprinkled with powdered sugar. Carefully peel off foil. Immediately roll cake in towel starting from narrow end; place on wire rack. Cool completely. Prepare Vanilla Cream Filling. Unroll cake; remove towel. Spread with filling; reroll cake. Spread Chocolate Glaze over top and sides. Cover; refrigerate until just before serving. Garnish with Vanilla Leaves and candied cherries, if desired. 10 to 12 servings.

VANILLA CREAM FILLING: In small bowl, sprinkle gelatin over cold water; let stand 1 minute to soften. In small microwave-safe bowl, combine vanilla chips and milk. Microwave at HIGH (100%) 30 seconds to 1 minute, stirring vigorously after 30 seconds, until chips are melted when stirred. Add gelatin mixture and vanilla extract; stir until gelatin is dissolved. Cool to room temperature. In small mixer bowl, beat whipping cream until stiff; carefully fold into vanilla mixture. Refrigerate 10 minutes or until filling begins to set. About 2 cups filling.

CHOCOLATE GLAZE: In small saucepan over low heat, melt butter; add cocoa and water, stirring until smooth and slightly thickened. Do *not* boil. Remove from heat; cool slightly. Gradually add powdered sugar and vanilla, beating with wire whisk until blended. About ¾ cup glaze.

Chocolate Glaze
   2 tablespoons butter or margarine
   2 tablespoons HERSHEY'S Cocoa
      or HERSHEY'S Premium
      European Style Cocoa
   2 tablespoons water
   1 cup powdered sugar
   ½ teaspoon vanilla extract

Chocolate Raspberry Mini Cakes

Heat oven to 350°F. Lightly spray four 5¾ x 3¼ x 2-inch foil loaf pans with no stick cooking spray. In small sauce-pan, over low heat, melt preserves, stirring constantly; set aside. In large mixer bowl, beat butter and sugar until blended. Add eggs and vanilla; beat well. Stir together flour, cocoa, baking soda, baking powder and salt; add to butter mixture alternately with butter-milk. Beat 2 minutes. Add preserves; beat until well blended. Pour batter evenly into prepared pans. Bake 25 to 30 minutes or until wooden pick inserted in center comes out clean. Cool completely in pans. Drizzle Vanilla Glaze in a random pattern over top. 4 cakes.

VANILLA GLAZE: In small saucepan, over low heat, melt butter. Add powdered sugar alternately with water, beating with wire whisk until smooth and of drizzling consistency. About ⅓ cup glaze.

* To sour milk: Use 1½ teaspoons white vinegar plus milk to equal ½ cup.

½ cup seedless red raspberry
   preserves
¼ cup butter or margarine,
   softened
½ cup sugar
2 eggs
1 teaspoon vanilla extract
1 cup all-purpose flour
⅓ cup HERSHEY'S Cocoa
¾ teaspoon baking soda
½ teaspoon baking powder
⅛ teaspoon salt
½ cup buttermilk or sour milk*
Vanilla Glaze

Vanilla Glaze
   2 tablespoons butter or margarine
   ⅔ cup powdered sugar
   2 to 3 teaspoons hot water

Chocolate Layered Angel Cake

1 box (14.5 oz.) angel food
  cake mix
¼ cup HERSHEY'S Cocoa or
  HERSHEY'S Premium
  European Style Cocoa
Chocolate Glaze

Chocolate Glaze
  ⅓ cup sugar
  ¼ cup water
  1 cup HERSHEY'S Semi-
    Sweet Chocolate Chips

Adjust oven rack to lowest position. Heat oven to 375°F. Prepare cake according to package directions. Measure 4 cups batter into separate bowl; gradually sift cocoa over this batter, folding until well blended, being careful not to deflate batter. Alternately spoon plain and chocolate batters into ungreased 10-inch tube pan. Bake 30 to 35 minutes or until top crust is firm and looks very dry. Do *not* underbake. Invert pan on heat-proof funnel or bottle; cool completely, at least 1½ hours. Carefully run knife along side of pan to loosen cake; remove from pan. Place on serving plate; drizzle with Chocolate Glaze. 18 servings.

CHOCOLATE GLAZE: In small saucepan, combine sugar and water. Cook over medium heat, stirring constantly, until mixture boils. Stir until sugar dissolves; remove from heat. Immediately add chocolate chips; stir until chips are melted and mixture is smooth. Cool to desired consistency; use immediately. About ⅔ cup glaze.

BAKER'S HINT

Angel or sponge-type cakes are cooled by inverting the pan. This allows the cake to cool without loosing volume. These cakes may be served with either side up.

Chocolate Layered Angel Cake

Cocoa Chiffon Cake

2 cups sugar, divided
1½ cups cake flour
⅔ cup HERSHEY'S Cocoa
2 teaspoons baking powder
1 teaspoon salt
½ teaspoon baking soda
½ cup vegetable oil
7 eggs, separated
¾ cup cold water
2 teaspoons vanilla extract
½ teaspoon cream of tartar
Vanilla Glaze

Vanilla Glaze
  ⅓ cup butter or margarine
  2 cups powdered sugar
  1½ teaspoons vanilla extract
  2 to 4 tablespoons hot water

Heat oven to 325°F. In large bowl, stir together 1¾ cups sugar, flour, cocoa, baking powder, salt and baking soda. Add oil, egg yolks, water and vanilla; beat until smooth. In large mixer bowl, beat egg whites and cream of tartar until soft peaks form. Gradually add remaining ¼ cup sugar, beating until stiff peaks form. Gradually pour chocolate batter over beaten egg whites, folding with rubber spatula just until blended. Pour into ungreased 10-inch tube pan. Bake 1 hour and 20 minutes or until top springs back when touched lightly. Invert pan on heat-proof funnel until completely cool. Remove cake from pan; invert onto serving plate. Spread top of cake with Vanilla Glaze, allowing some to drizzle down sides. 12 to 16 servings.

VANILLA GLAZE: In medium saucepan over low heat, melt butter. Remove from heat. Stir in powdered sugar and vanilla. Stir in water, 1 tablespoon at a time, until smooth and of desired consistency. About 1¼ cups glaze.

Harvest Cakes

Fresh Apple Mini Chip Cake

3 eggs

1 cup vegetable oil

½ cup bottled apple juice

2 teaspoons vanilla extract

3 cups all-purpose flour

1¾ cups sugar

½ teaspoon ground cinnamon

1 teaspoon baking soda

¾ teaspoon salt

3 cups diced, peeled tart apples

1 cup HERSHEY'S MINI CHIPS
Semi-Sweet Chocolate

¾ cup finely chopped nuts

Cream Cheese Frosting

Additional HERSHEY'S MINI
CHIPS Semi-Sweet Chocolate
(optional)

Cream Cheese Frosting

   1 package (3 oz.) cream cheese,
     softened

   2 tablespoons butter or
     margarine, softened

   2 cups powdered sugar

   1 teaspoon vanilla extract

Heat oven to 350°F. Grease and flour two 9-inch round baking pans. In large bowl, beat eggs slightly; stir in oil, apple juice and vanilla. Stir together flour, sugar, cinnamon, baking soda and salt; stir into batter until smooth. Add apples, 1 cup small chocolate chips and nuts; stir until evenly mixed. Pour batter into prepared pans. Bake 40 to 45 minutes or until wooden pick inserted in center comes out clean. Cool 10 minutes; remove from pans to wire racks. Cool completely. Prepare Cream Cheese Frosting. Spread one-half frosting on bottom layer; top with second layer. Spread remaining frosting on top of cake. Garnish with additional small chocolate chips, if desired. 10 to 12 servings.

CREAM CHEESE FROSTING: In small mixer bowl, beat cream cheese and butter until smooth and well blended. Gradually add powdered sugar; stir in vanilla. Beat until smooth (1 to 2 teaspoons milk may be added for desired spreading consistency). About 1 cup frosting.

VARIATION

Fluted Tube Pan: Bake in well greased and floured 12-cup fluted tube pan 1 hour and 5 to 15 minutes.

13 x 9 x 2-inch Baking Pan: Bake in well greased and floured 13 x 9 x 2-inch baking pan 35 to 40 minutes.

Chocolatey Fresh Apple Cake, Fresh Apple Mini Chip Cake

Chocolatey Fresh Apple Cake

2¾ cups all-purpose flour
2 cups granulated sugar
⅔ cup HERSHEY'S Cocoa
1½ teaspoons baking soda
½ teaspoon baking powder
1 teaspoon ground cinnamon
¾ teaspoon salt
3 eggs
1 cup buttermilk or sour milk*
1 cup vegetable oil
2 teaspoons vanilla extract
2 cups shredded peeled tart
   apples, drained**
1 cup finely chopped nuts
Powdered sugar or Chocolate Glaze

Chocolate Glaze
   2 tablespoons butter
      or margarine
   2 tablespoons HERSHEY'S
      Cocoa
   2 tablespoons water
   1 cup powdered sugar
   1 teaspoon vanilla extract

Heat oven to 350°F. Grease and flour 12-cup fluted tube pan. Stir together flour, granulated sugar, cocoa, baking soda, baking powder, cinnamon and salt; set aside. In large mixer bowl, combine eggs, buttermilk, oil and vanilla; beat on low speed of electric mixer until blended. Gradually add dry ingredients; stir in apples and nuts until evenly mixed. Pour batter into prepared pan. Bake 60 to 65 minutes or until wooden pick inserted in center of cake comes out clean. Cool 10 minutes. Remove from pan to wire rack. Cool completely. Sprinkle top with powdered sugar or drizzle with Chocolate Glaze. 10 to 12 servings.

CHOCOLATE GLAZE: In small saucepan over low heat, melt butter. Add cocoa and water, stirring constantly until mixture thickens. Do not boil. Remove from heat; gradually beat in powdered sugar and vanilla until smooth and of glazing consistency. Add additional water, ½ teaspoon at a time, if necessary. About ½ cup glaze.

* To sour milk: Use 1 tablespoon white vinegar plus milk to equal 1 cup.

** Shred in food processor, if available.

Easy Pumpkin Cake

Heat oven to 350°F. Grease and flour 12-cup fluted tube pan. In large mixer bowl, stir together dry cake mix, pumpkin pie spice, baking soda, pumpkin, water, oil and eggs; beat on low speed of electric mixer until moistened. Beat on medium speed 2 minutes until smooth. Stir in small chocolate chips. Pour batter into prepared pan. Bake 45 to 50 minutes or until top springs back when touched lightly. Cool 10 minutes; remove from pan to wire rack. Cool completely. Drizzle Chocolate Glaze over top of cake; sprinkle with nuts, if desired. 12 to 16 servings.

CHOCOLATE GLAZE: In small saucepan, stir together sugar and water. Cook over medium heat, stirring constantly, until mixture boils and sugar is dissolved. Remove from heat; immediately add small chocolate chips, stirring until melted. Continue stirring until glaze is desired consistency.

1 package (about 18.25 oz.) yellow cake mix
3 to 4 teaspoons ground pumpkin pie spice
2 teaspoons baking soda
1¾ cups (16-oz. can) pumpkin
¼ cup water
¼ cup vegetable oil
3 eggs
1 cup HERSHEY'S MINI CHIPS Semi-Sweet Chocolate
Chocolate Glaze
Chopped nuts (optional)

Chocolate Glaze
2 tablespoons sugar
2 tablespoons water
½ cup HERSHEY'S MINI CHIPS Semi-Sweet Chocolate

Glazed Cranberry Mini Cakes, Cocoa Fruit Cake

Cocoa Fruit Cake

Heat oven to 325°F. Grease and flour 12-cup fluted tube pan. In large mixer bowl, beat butter, sugar, vanilla and brandy extract until light and fluffy. Add eggs; beat well. Stir together flour, cocoa, salt and baking powder; add alternately with buttermilk to butter mixture, beating just until blended. Stir together cherries, nuts, raisins and mixed fruit; fold into batter. Pour batter into prepared pan. Bake 1 hour and 25 minutes or until wooden pick inserted in center comes out clean. Cool 10 minutes; remove from pan. Immediately wrap in foil. Allow to stand overnight before serving. To serve, sprinkle powdered sugar over top, if desired. 12 to 16 servings.

* To sour milk: Use 1½ teaspoons white vinegar plus milk to equal ½ cup.

¾ cup (1½ sticks) butter or
  margarine, softened
1½ cups sugar
½ teaspoon vanilla extract
¼ teaspoon brandy extract
3 eggs
1 cup all-purpose flour
6 tablespoons HERSHEY'S Cocoa
½ teaspoon salt
¼ teaspoon baking powder
½ cup buttermilk or sour milk*
2 cups candied red cherries,
  cut in half
1½ cups pecans, coarsely chopped
1 cup golden raisins
½ cup chopped, mixed
  candied fruit
Powdered sugar (optional)

Powdered sugar may be used as a quick and easy garnish for an unfrosted cake. Place powdered sugar in a sieve; shake sieve gently to dust top of cake with sugar. For variety, use small amount of cocoa mixed with the sugar or place small stencil or doily on cake surface, dust with sugar and carefully remove stencil. The design will be outlined with sugar.

BAKER'S HINT

Glazed Cranberry Mini Cakes

⅓ cup butter or margarine,
   softened
⅓ cup granulated sugar
⅓ cup packed light brown sugar
1 egg
1¼ teaspoons vanilla extract
1⅓ cups all-purpose flour
¾ teaspoon baking powder
¼ teaspoon baking soda
¼ teaspoon salt
2 tablespoons milk
1¼ cups coarsely chopped
   fresh cranberries
½ cup coarsely chopped walnuts
⅔ cup HERSHEY'S Vanilla
   Milk Chips
Vanilla Glaze

Vanilla Glaze
   1 cup HERSHEY'S Vanilla
      Milk Chips
   2 tablespoons vegetable oil

Heat oven to 350°F. Lightly grease or paper-line small muffin cups (1¾ inches in diameter). In small mixer bowl, beat butter, granulated sugar, brown sugar, egg and vanilla extract until light and fluffy. Stir together flour, baking powder, baking soda and salt; gradually mix into butter mixture. Add milk; stir until blended. Stir in cranberries, walnuts and vanilla milk chips. Fill muffin cups about ⅞ full with batter. Bake 18 to 20 minutes or until wooden pick inserted in center comes out clean. Cool 5 minutes; remove from pans to wire racks. Cool completely. Prepare Vanilla Glaze; drizzle glaze on tops. Place on wax paper-covered tray; refrigerate 10 minutes to set glaze. About 3 dozen mini cakes.

VANILLA GLAZE: In small microwave-safe bowl, place vanilla milk chips; sprinkle oil over chips. Microwave at HIGH (100%) 30 seconds; stir vigorously. If necessary, microwave at HIGH additional 30 seconds or just until chips are melted when stirred.

Carrot Cake

Heat oven to 350°F. Grease and flour 13 x 9 x 2-inch baking pan. In large bowl, stir together flour, granulated sugar, brown sugar, baking soda, cinnamon and salt. In small bowl, stir together eggs, oil and vanilla; stir into dry ingredients, blending well. Stir in carrot, peanut butter chips and walnuts. Pour batter into prepared pan. Bake 35 to 40 minutes or until wooden pick inserted in center comes out clean. Cool completely in pan on wire rack. Frost with Cream Cheese Frosting. Garnish with walnuts, if desired. 12 to 15 servings.

CREAM CHEESE FROSTING: In small mixer bowl, beat cream cheese and butter until well blended. Gradually add powdered sugar and vanilla, beating to spreading consistency.

1½ cups all-purpose flour

¾ cup granulated sugar

½ cup packed light brown sugar

1¼ teaspoons baking soda

1 teaspoon ground cinnamon

½ teaspoon salt

3 eggs

¾ cup vegetable oil

1½ teaspoons vanilla extract

2 cups shredded carrot

1⅔ cups (10-oz. pkg.) REESE'S Peanut Butter Chips *or* 2 cups (12-oz. pkg.) HERSHEY'S Semi-Sweet Chocolate Chips *or* HERSHEY'S MINI CHIPS Semi-Sweet Chocolate

½ cup chopped walnuts

Cream Cheese Frosting

Chopped walnuts (optional)

Cream Cheese Frosting

   1 package (3 oz.) cream cheese, softened

   ¼ cup (½ stick) butter or margarine, softened

   2 cups powdered sugar

   1 teaspoon vanilla extract

Crunchy Topped Cocoa Cake

1 ½ cups all-purpose flour
1 cup sugar
¼ cup HERSHEY'S Cocoa
1 teaspoon baking soda
½ teaspoon salt
1 cup water
¼ cup plus 2 tablespoons
   vegetable oil
1 tablespoon white vinegar
1 teaspoon vanilla extract
Broiled Topping

Broiled Topping
  ¼ cup (½ stick) butter or
    margarine, softened
  ½ cup packed light
    brown sugar
  ½ cup coarsely chopped nuts
  ½ cup flaked coconut
  3 tablespoons light cream or
    evaporated milk

Heat oven to 350°F. Grease and flour 8-inch square baking pan. In large bowl, stir together flour, sugar, cocoa, baking soda and salt. Add water, oil, vinegar and vanilla; beat with spoon or wire whisk just until batter is smooth and ingredients are well blended. Pour batter into prepared pan. Bake 35 to 40 minutes or until wooden pick inserted in center comes out clean. Meanwhile, prepare Broiled Topping; spread on warm cake. Set oven to Broil; place cake about 4 inches from heat. Broil 3 minutes or until top is bubbly and golden brown. Remove from oven; cool completely in pan on wire rack. 9 servings.

BROILED TOPPING: In small bowl, stir together all ingredients until well blended.

Crunchy Topped Cocoa Cake, Streusel Apple Spice Cake

Streusel Apple – Spice Cake

½ cup (1 stick) butter or
   margarine, softened
1 cup sugar
2 eggs
1 teaspoon vanilla extract
2¼ cups all-purpose flour
¾ teaspoon baking powder
¾ teaspoon ground cinnamon
½ teaspoon baking soda
¼ teaspoon ground cloves
⅛ teaspoon salt
¾ cup milk
½ cups chopped, peeled tart
   apples
¾ cup HERSHEY'S MINI
   CHIPS Semi-Sweet Chocolate
Streusel Topping
Semi-Sweet Chocolate Glaze
   (optional)

Streusel Topping
   ⅓ cup all-purpose flour
   3 tablespoons sugar
   2 tablespoons butter or
      margarine

Semi-Sweet Chocolate Glaze (optional)
   3 tablespoons HERSHEY'S
      MINI CHIPS Semi-Sweet
      Chocolate
   ½ teaspoon shortening

Heat oven to 350°F. Grease 9 x 5 x 3-inch loaf pan. In large mixer bowl, beat butter and sugar until light and fluffy. Add eggs and vanilla; beat well. Stir together flour, baking powder, cinnamon, baking soda, cloves and salt; add alternately with milk to butter mixture, blending well. Gently fold in apples and ¾ cup small chocolate chips. Spoon batter into prepared pan. Prepare Streusel Topping; sprinkle on top of batter in pan. Bake 1 hour and 10 to 15 minutes or until wooden pick inserted in center comes out clean. Cool 10 minutes; remove from pan to wire rack. Turn right side up. Drizzle Semi-Sweet Chocolate Glaze over top. Allow glaze to set before cutting cake. 12 servings.

STREUSEL TOPPING: In small bowl, stir together flour and sugar; cut in butter to form fine crumbs.

SEMI-SWEET CHOCOLATE GLAZE: In small microwave-safe bowl, place chocolate chips and shortening. Microwave at HIGH (100%) 30 to 45 seconds or until chips are melted when stirred.

Cocoa Zucchini Cake

Heat oven to 350°F. Grease and flour 13 x 9 x 2-inch baking pan. Place zucchini in sieve; press zucchini to remove moisture (discard liquid). In large mixer bowl, beat eggs, sugar, oil and vanilla until thick. Stir together flour, cocoa, baking soda, baking powder, salt, cinnamon and cloves; add to egg mixture, beating just until well blended. Stir in zucchini and walnuts. Spoon batter into prepared pan. Bake 35 to 40 minutes or until cake begins to pull away from sides of pan. Cool in pan on wire rack. Drizzle Cream Cheese Glaze over top. Cut into squares. About 15 servings.

CREAM CHEESE GLAZE: In small mixer bowl, beat cream cheese until fluffy. Gradually add powdered sugar, beating until well blended. Beat in vanilla and water. Add butter; beat until smooth.

2 cups shredded unpeeled
  raw zucchini
3 eggs
1½ cups sugar
1¼ cups vegetable oil
1½ teaspoons vanilla extract
2 cups all-purpose flour
⅓ cup HERSHEY'S Cocoa
2 teaspoons baking soda
1 teaspoon baking powder
½ teaspoon salt
1 teaspoon ground cinnamon
¼ teaspoon ground cloves
¾ cup chopped walnuts
Cream Cheese Glaze

Cream Cheese Glaze
  1½ ounces cream cheese (½ of
    3-oz. pkg.), softened
  1 cup powdered sugar
  ½ teaspoon vanilla extract
  1 tablespoon hot water
  2 tablespoons butter or
    margarine, melted

Halloween Pumpkin Torte

Harvest Pumpkin Torte

Heat oven to 375°F. Line 15½ x 10½ x 1-inch jelly roll pan with foil; generously grease foil. In large mixer bowl, beat egg yolks on medium speed of electric mixer 3 minutes; gradually add ½ cup sugar, beating 2 additional minutes. Stir together flour, cocoa, ¼ cup sugar, baking soda and salt; add to egg yolk mixture alternately with water, beating on low speed just until batter is smooth. Stir in vanilla; set aside. In small mixer bowl, beat egg whites until soft peaks form; gradually add remaining 1 tablespoon sugar, beating until stiff peaks form. Gradually fold beaten egg whites into chocolate mixture until well blended. Spread batter evenly into prepared pan. Bake 14 to 16 minutes or until top springs back when touched lightly. Immediately loosen cake from edges of pan; invert onto clean, slightly dampened towel. Carefully peel off foil. Cool completely. Meanwhile, prepare Pumpkin Filling.Cut cake crosswise into four equal pieces. Place one piece on serving plate; spread about ¾ cup Pumpkin Filling over top. Repeat layering with remaining cake and filling, ending with cake layer. Spread Chocolate Glaze over top; garnish with almonds, if desired. Refrigerate until serving time. 8 to 10 servings.

PUMPKIN FILLING: In small saucepan, combine pumpkin and flour; cook over medium heat, stirring constantly, until mixture boils (mixture will be very thick). Remove from heat; set aside. Cool completely. In small mixer bowl, beat butter and shortening until creamy; add spices. Gradually add powdered sugar, beating until light and fluffy. Slowly blend in pumpkin mixture. Refrigerate until ready to use. About 2¼ cups filling.

4 eggs, separated
¾ cup plus 1 tablespoon sugar, divided
½ cup all-purpose flour
⅓ cup HERSHEY'S Cocoa
½ teaspoon baking soda
¼ teaspoon salt
⅓ cup water
1 teaspoon vanilla extract
Pumpkin Filling
Chocolate Glaze
Slivered almonds (optional)

Pumpkin Filling
1 cup canned pumpkin
¼ cup all-purpose flour
⅓ cup butter or margarine, softened
3 tablespoons shortening
1 teaspoon ground cinnamon
¼ teaspoon ground nutmeg
1¾ cups powdered sugar

Chocolate Glaze
- 1 tablespoon butter or margarine
- 2 tablespoons HERSHEY'S Cocoa
- 1 tablespoon water
- ⅔ cup powdered sugar
- ¼ teaspoon vanilla extract

CHOCOLATE GLAZE: In small saucepan over low heat, melt butter; add cocoa and water. Cook, stirring constantly, until mixture thickens. Do not boil. Remove from heat; gradually add powdered sugar and vanilla, beating with wire whisk until smooth. Add additional water, ½ teaspoon at a time, until of desired consistency. About ½ cup glaze.

Chocolate Raisin Snacking Cake

- ¾ cup raisins
- 1 cup water
- 1¼ cups granulated sugar
- ⅔ cup vegetable oil
- 1 egg, slightly beaten
- 1¾ cups all-purpose flour
- ⅓ cup HERSHEY'S Cocoa
- 1 teaspoon baking soda
- ½ teaspoon salt
- ¼ teaspoon ground cinnamon
- ½ cup chopped nuts
- Powdered sugar

Heat oven to 350°F. Grease and flour 13 x 9 x 2-inch baking pan. In medium saucepan, heat raisins and water to boiling; simmer 1 minute. Remove from heat; cool slightly. Stir in granultated sugar and oil. Add egg; stir until well blended. Stir together flour, cocoa, baking soda, salt and cinnamon; stir into raisin mixture, blending well. Stir in nuts. Pour batter into prepared pan. Bake 25 to 30 minutes or until wooden pick inserted in center comes out clean. Sprinkle powdered sugar over warm cake. Cool in pan on wire rack. 15 servings.

Kids Cakes

Cocoa Party Cake

Cocoa Party Cake

Heat oven to 350°F. Grease and flour three 9-inch round baking pans, or one 13 x 9 x 2-inch baking pan. In large mixer bowl, beat butter, sugar and vanilla until light and fluffy. Add eggs; beat well. Stir together flour, cocoa, baking soda and salt; add alternately with buttermilk to butter mixture. Pour batter into prepared pans. Bake 30 to 35 minutes for round pans, 55 to 60 minutes for rectangular pan or until wooden pick inserted in center comes out clean. Cool 10 minutes; remove from pans. Cool completely. Frost as desired. 12 servings.

* To sour milk: Use 2 tablespoons white vinegar plus milk to equal 2 cups.

1 cup (2 sticks) butter or
  margarine, softened
2¼ cups sugar
1 teaspoon vanilla extract
2 eggs
2¾ cups cake flour
½ cup HERSHEY'S Cocoa
2 teaspoons baking soda
1 teaspoon salt
2 cups buttermilk or sour milk*

Brush cake layers before frosting to remove any excess crumbs. Place the bottom layer upside down on serving plate. Spread flat surface with frosting. Place the top cake layer right side up. Spread remaining frosting on sides and top of cake.

BAKER'S HINT

Easy Peanutty Bunny

1⅔ cups (10-oz. pkg.) REESE'S
  Peanut Butter Chips
1 tablespoon shortening
1 package (about 18.5 oz.) regular
  yellow cake mix (*not* pudding-
  in-mix type)

To Decorate:
  1 can (16.5 oz.) ready-to-spread
    creamy vanilla frosting
  ½ cup flaked coconut
  1 marshmallow, halved (ears)
  2 HERSHEY'S Milk
    Chocolate Kisses (pupils)
  1 pink square mint (nose)
  2 squares candy coated gum
    (teeth)
  6 4-inch strands red
    shoestring licorice (whiskers)
  REESE'S Peanut Butter Chips
    (optional)

Heat oven to 350°F. Grease and wax-paper line two 9-inch round baking pans. In microwave-safe bowl, place peanut butter chips and shortening. Microwave at HIGH (100%) 1½ minutes or until smooth when stirred. Prepare cake mix with water and eggs as directed on package; blend in melted peanut butter chip mixture. Pour batter into prepared pans. Bake 30 to 35 minutes or until wooden pick inserted in center comes out clean. Cool 10 minutes; remove from pans to wire racks. Cool completely. Cut cake and decorate as follows.

To Form Bunny: Following the attached diagram, cut 1 cake layer to form bunny ears, about 6 x 1 inches. Place cut layer next to second to form bunny head and body. Place "ears" on top.

To Decorate: Frost bunny; sprinkle with coconut. Form ears, eyes, nose, teeth and whiskers as shown in diagram.

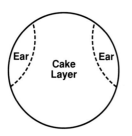

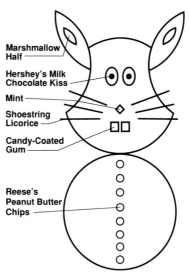

Easy Peanutty Bunny

Miss Molly Moo From Dairyland View

Miss Molly Moo From Dairyland View

Heat oven to 350°F. Grease and flour two 9-inch round baking pans. In large mixer bowl, stir together sugar, flour, cocoa, baking powder, baking soda and salt. Add eggs, milk, oil and vanilla; beat on medium speed of electric mixer 2 minutes. Remove from mixer; stir in boiling water (batter will be thin). Pour batter into prepared pans. Bake 30 to 35 minutes or until wooden pick inserted in center comes out clean. Cool 10 minutes; remove from pans to wire rack. Cool completely. Prepare Brown and White Frosting.

To form Miss Molly Moo: Place one cake layer on serving platter. Spread top with White Frosting. Top with second cake layer. Following the diagram, form ears by cutting long ovals from each side of cake, being careful not to cut through top of circle. Gently move ears up slightly from side of face. Frost cake sides and face with brown and white frosting as shown in photograph. Using Brown Frosting, pipe on eyes, nostrils and a big smile. 10 to 12 servings.

BROWN AND WHITE FROSTING: In large mixer bowl, beat butter until fluffy. Add powdered sugar alternately with 4 tablespoons milk; beat until spreading consistency. Blend in vanilla. Remove 2 cups frosting. Add cocoa and 2 tablespoons milk to remaining frosting; beat until thoroughly blended.

2 cups sugar
1¾ cups all-purpose flour
¾ cup HERSHEY'S Cocoa
1½ teaspoons baking powder
1½ teaspoons baking soda
1 teaspoon salt
2 eggs
1 cup milk
½ cup vegetable oil
2 teaspoons vanilla extract
1 cup boiling water
Brown and White Frosting

Brown and White Frosting
1 cup (2 sticks) butter or
   margarine, divided
6 cups powdered sugar
6 tablespoons milk, divided
2 teaspoons vanilla extract
½ cup HERSHEY'S Cocoa

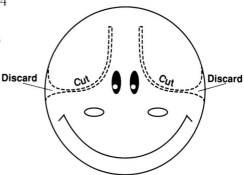

Chocolate Stripe Cake

Heat oven to 350°F. Line 13 x 9 x 2-inch baking pan with foil; grease and flour foil. Prepare cake batter and bake according to package directions. Cool 15 minutes; do *not* remove cake from pan. With end of drinking straw, carefully pierce down through cake to bottom of pan; make rows about 1 inch apart covering length and width of cake. In small bowl, sprinkle gelatin over cold water; let stand 1 minute to soften. Add boiling water; stir until gelatin is completely dissolved and mixture is clear. Stir in syrup. Pour chocolate mixture evenly over cooled cake, making sure entire top is covered and mixture has flowed into holes. Cover; refrigerate about 5 hours or until set. Remove cake from pan; peel off foil. Spread with Chocolate Syrup Whipped Cream Frosting or whipped topping. Cover; refrigerate leftovers. 12 to 15 servings.

CHOCOLATE SYRUP WHIPPED CREAM FROSTING: In small mixer bowl, stir together whipping cream and powdered sugar. Beat on high speed of electric mixer until stiff; stir in syrup. Cover; refrigerate until ready to spread on cake. About 2½ cups frosting.

VARIATION
STRAWBERRY SYRUP WHIPPED CREAM FROSTING:
Use ¼ cup HERSHEY'S Strawberry Flavored Syrup instead of HERSHEY'S Syrup.

1 package (about 18.25 oz.) white
  cake mix
1 envelope unflavored gelatin
¼ cup cold water
¼ cup boiling water
1 cup HERSHEY'S Syrup
Chocolate Syrup Whipped Cream
  Frosting or Whipped topping

*Chocolate Syrup Whipped
Cream Frosting*
  1½ cups cold whipping
    cream
  2 tablespoons powdered sugar
  ¼ cup HERSHEY'S Syrup

Peanut Butter Party Cones, Chocolate Stripe Cake

Peanut Butter Party Cones

Heat oven to 350°F. Prepare cake batter according to package directions; set aside. In saucepan over low heat, melt peanut butter chips with milk, stirring constantly until blended. Add peanut butter mixture while warm to cake batter. Beat on medium speed of electric mixer until blended, about 2 minutes. Fill ice cream cone cups ⅔ to ¾ full with batter. Place upright in regular muffin cups or 2 inches apart on cookie sheet. Bake 30 to 35 minutes or until wooden pick inserted comes out clean. Cool completely. Frost as desired. Decorate with chocolate or colored candy sprinkles. 24 cones.

1 package (about 18.25 oz.) yellow cake mix
1½ cups REESE'S Peanut Butter Chips
½ cup milk
24 waffle-type ice cream cones with flat bottoms
Two 16-ounce containers any flavor ready-to-spread frosting
Chocolate or colored candy sprinkles

Chocolate Banana Snack Cake

Heat oven to 350°F. Grease and flour 8-inch square baking pan. In small bowl, stir together flour, sugar, cocoa, baking soda and salt. Add water, oil, vinegar and vanilla; beat with spoon or wire whisk until smooth. Stir in banana. Sprinkle chocolate chips over top. Bake 35 to 40 minutes or until wooden pick inserted in center comes out clean. Cool completely in pan on wire rack. Cut into squares. 6 to 8 servings.

1⅔ cups all-purpose flour

1 cup packed light brown sugar

¼ cup HERSHEY'S Cocoa

1 teaspoon baking soda

¼ teaspoon salt

½ cup water

⅓ cup vegetable oil

1 teaspoon white vinegar

¾ teaspoon vanilla extract

½ cup mashed, ripe banana (1 medium banana)

½ cup HERSHEY'S Semi-Sweet Chocolate Chips

Chocolate Triangles & Wedges

In microwave-safe bowl, place chocolate chips. Microwave at HIGH (100%) 1 minute; stir. Microwave at HIGH an additional 15 seconds at a time, stirring after each heating, just until chocolate is melted when stirred. On wax paper-covered cookie sheet spread melted chocolate with spatula into 8-inch square or circle. Chill 5 to 8 minutes or just until chocolate begins to set.

With sharp knife score chocolate square into smaller squares; cut each small square diagonally in half to make triangles. Score chocolate circle into pie-like wedges. Do not try to separate at this time. Cover; chill several hours or until very firm. Carefully peel wax paper away from chocolate; gently separate triangles or wedges at score marks. Place on tray; cover and refrigerate until ready to use.

1 cup HERSHEY'S Semi-Sweet Chocolate Chips

Rosettes

In small mixer bowl, stir together sugar and cocoa. Stir in whipping cream and vanilla. Beat until stiff. Fit decorating bag with large rosette tip; spoon chocolate cream into bag. Pipe rosettes on top of ice cream cake.

¼ cup sugar
2 tablespoons HERSHEY'S Cocoa
½ cup cold whipping cream
½ teaspoon vanilla extract

Chocolate Curls

HERSHEY'S Milk Chocolate Bar,
SPECIAL DARK Bar, or
Unsweetened Baking Chocolate

The secret to successful curls is chocolate at the proper temperature, slightly warm but still firm. On a warm day, room temperature might be fine. Place unwrapped chocolate on cookie sheet. Place in cooled oven until warm. (Or Microwave at High (100%) about 30 seconds or just until chocolate feels slightly warm.) With even pressure draw vegetable peeler along underside of chocolate; a curl will form. Use wooden pick to lift curl onto wax paper-covered tray. Refrigerate until firm.

Use side of candy bar for narrow curls. Use width of one or two blocks for medium-size curls. Use entire width of bar for large curls.

Chocolate Filigree Hearts

2 cups (12-oz. pkg.)
HERSHEY'S Semi-Sweet
Chocolate Chips

Draw desired size heart shapes on paper; cover with wax or parchment paper. Place both sheets of paper on baking sheet or tray. In microwave-safe bowl, place chocolate chips. Microwave at HIGH (100% power) 1 to 1½ minutes or until chips are melted when stirred. Place chocolate in small pastry bag fitted with writing tip on wax paper, following heart outlines, pipe chocolate into heart shapes. Fill in center of hearts with a crisscross of chocolate to connect the sides. Refrigerate until hearts are firm. Carefully peel wax paper away from chocolate hearts. Place on tray. Refrigerate until ready to use.

Chocolate Leaves

Thoroughly wash and dry leaves. In small microwave-safe bowl, place ½ cup HERSHEY'S Semi-Sweet Chocolate Chips and 1 teaspoon vegetable shortening. Microwave at HIGH (100%) 45 seconds to 1 minute or until chips are melted when stirred. With small soft-bristled brush, brush melted chocolate onto backs of leaves being careful not to drip over edges; place on wax-paper covered tray or rack. Refrigerate until very firm. Carefully peel fresh leaves from chocolate leaves; refrigerate until ready to use.

Several ivy, lemon, rose or other non-toxic leaves
½ cup HERSHEY'S Semi-Sweet Chocolate Chips
1 teaspoon vegetable shortening

Vanilla Leaves

Thoroughly wash and dry several leaves. In small microwave-safe bowl, place vanilla chips and shortening. Microwave at HIGH (100%) 45 seconds to 1 minute or until chips are melted when stirred. With small soft-bristled pastry brush, brush melted vanilla chips onto backs of leaves, being careful not to drip over edges; place on wax paper-covered tray or rack. Refrigerate until very firm. Carefully peel fresh leaves from vanilla leaves; refrigerate until ready to use.

Several rose, lemon or other non-toxic leaves
½ cup HERSHEY'S Vanilla Milk Chips
1 teaspoon shortening

Chocolate Coated Ice Cream Cone

In small microwave-safe bowl, place chocolate chips and shortening. Microwave on HIGH (100%) 1 to 1½ minutes or just until chips are melted and mixture is smooth when stirred. Spoon melted chocolate over outside of flat-bottom ice cream cone. Refrigerate until chocolate is firm, about 30 minutes.

Unsweetened Baking Chocolate
1 cup HERSHEY'S Semi-Sweet Chocolate Chips
1 tablespoon shortening (not butter, margarine or oil)
Flat-bottom ice cream cone

Index